ALSO BY
STEVE BIDDULPH

The Secret of Happy Children
Raising Boys
Manhood

with SHAARON BIDDULPH
Love, Laughter and Parenting
How Love Works
The Making of Love

More SECRETS *of* HAPPY CHILDREN

How to Put Your Love into Action
and Raise Strong, Confident
and Loving Children

STEVE BIDDULPH
with Shaaron Biddulph

Illustrations by Paul Stanish
Cartoons by Allan Stomann

◆

Marlowe & Company
New York

MORE SECRETS OF HAPPY CHILDREN: *How to Put Your Love into Action and Raise Strong, Confident and Loving Children*

Copyright © Steve and Shaaron Biddulph 1994, 1998, 2003

Published by
Marlowe & Company
An Imprint of Avalon Publishing Group Incorporated
161 William Street, 16th Floor
New York, NY 10038

Originally published in Australia by Bay Books.
This edition published by arrangement with
HarperCollins Publishers Pty Limited.

Library of Congress Cataloging-in-Publication Data
Biddulph, Steve.
[More secrets of happy children]
More secrets of happy children : how to put your love into action
and raise strong, confident, and loving children /
Steve and Shaaron Biddulph.
Originally published under title: More secrets of happy children.
Sequel to: The secret of happy children.
ISBN 1-56924-488-X (pbk.)
1. Child rearing. 2. Parent and child. I. Biddulph, Shaaron.
II. Biddulph, Steve. Secret of happy children. III. Title.
HQ769.B572 2003
649'.1–dc21   2002045525

ISBN 1-56924-488-X

9   8   7   6   5   4   3   2   1

Designed by Pauline Neuwirth, Neuwirth and Associates, Inc.

Printed in the United States of America
Distributed by Publishers Group West

Contents

✦

Acknowledgments

✦

Thanks TO PHILLIPA SANDALL, Carolyn Walsh, and Robin Freeman for helping bring this book about. Paul Stanish skillfully redrew our cartoon ideas into something less squiggly. Matthew Lore brought the book to the United States, and Suzanne McCloskey helped us translate it into American English!

I am indebted beyond words to my partner, Shaaron Biddulph, for her wise way with kids, and the help she brings to my clumsy way of both parenting and writing.

Our own family grew up from babies to young adults during the life of this book, and so many people helped us to survive, learn, and grow. So thanks!

Thanks to *ITA* magazine for permission to quote Kirsty Cockburn; Boxtree Limited for permission to quote from *Are Mothers Really Necessary?* by Bob Mullen; Rosie Lever for permission to quote from *Such Sweet Sorrow*; Christopher Green for permission to quote from *Toddler Taming*; *Readers' Digest* magazine for permission to quote from Karl Zinsmeister's article, "Hard Truths About Day Care"; the Australian Institute of Family Studies, especially Gay Ochiltree for her book, *Children in Australian Families*; the *Melbourne Age* and Mary Burbridge for permission to use in full her article, "My Daughter, My Forever Baby"; the *Mercury* for permission to reproduce the Benjamin

Spock quote and the material on working mothers; the library staff at the Institute for Early Childhood Development at Kew, Melbourne, for their help and research facilities.

Introduction

✦

It's BEEN FOURTEEN years since I wrote my first book
on parenting. My life has been greatly affected by people's
responses to *The Secret of Happy Children* over those years.
Whenever Shaaron and I travel around the world, it is like meeting friends who already know us. The confidence that people
put in us makes us both proud and anxious. What inspires us is
the fact that people everywhere care SO much about their kids.

Parenthood is deep water. It can occasionally make you happier than anything else in your life, but you will also sometimes
feel like your heart is being put through the wringer! Don't let
anyone tell you that it is simple.

Today there are dozens of parenting books on the shelves.
These books have an odd effect on me—they make me feel ill!
So logical and cheerful! Full of breezy advice and long tidy lists
of what to do. Four steps to confident kids! Who are they kid-
ding? I prefer to live in the real world.

On the other hand, something has to be done—since many
parents are desperate for answers. So, where does this second
book fit in? It is a deeper book than the first one. It is also more
specific, since it is based on work with thousands more parents
who have told us what works. The ideas of softlove and firmlove, which you'll learn about in this book, are powerful tools

that can turn family life around. They address the real aims of parenthood—to produce young adults with warm hearts and lots of backbone.

There are also two big challenges for mothers and fathers embedded in this book:

- ✦ to give up violence and fear-based methods of discipline
- ✦ to really raise your own children, and not leave this job to others

It's clear that raising kids sends you on an inner journey of self-discovery. This is certainly worthwhile. So—no quick answers in this book. Instead, some powerful ideas to help you find "your own right way."

Much love to your family from ours,

Steve Biddulph

P.S. The wombats have grown up and left home!

Experts can be a hazard to your family's health.
Luckily, this is a nonexpert book!
Please take it for what it is—friendly suggestions,
and support for your own good sense.

In your heart,
YOU know what's right
for you and your children.

More
SECRETS OF HAPPY CHILDREN

one

Making Tomorrow's People

◆

Imagine THIS. You are sitting on the front porch. In front of you are gardens and a leafy street—there is no sound but the singing of birds. You are old, but still tanned and fit, and wearing warm, soft clothes.

A sleek and almost silent vehicle rolls up. Its doors click open, and some young adults step out. They are your grown-up children!

They give you big hugs. They are full of energy, and happy to see you. They sit down and tell you their latest adventures, new achievements, and news of their families. You bring out food and drinks, and talk over many things. Eventually, it's time for them to leave.

You go inside and put on a warm sweater.

For a long time you sit by the window, remembering back to when they were children. You feel very proud of how they have turned out, of what you have given the world.

SEEING YOUR KIDS AS A GIFT

IF YOU WERE to believe the media, you'd think that kids are nothing but one big problem—a behavior problem, a child-care problem, a health problem.

This is a terrible con, because the truth is—kids are a beautiful gift. Deep down we really know this, but sometimes we forget. The one couple in five who have fertility problems know what a gift children are. So do the parents whose children battle illness or disability. When our children are endangered, we suddenly realize that they matter so much, and that other things matter so little.

There are real challenges in raising kids. In this book we'll tackle many of these. But you should start by reminding yourself what a fantastic thing you have in your life—the shaping of a new life, the launching of a wonderful human being into the future. You will give and receive. Your life will be greatly enriched by the love and adoration you can receive from your children, who approach everything with freshness, intensity, and trust.

We are now raising twenty-first-century children, and are actually doing quite well—creating a kind of young person who is light years ahead of the young adults of thirty years ago. (Compare yourself at fifteen, say, with what fifteen-year-olds are like now!)

Raising kids is an ancient craft. To do it well you have to discover your hidden inner resources, as well as draw on many outer supports. You adopt a kind of "finding the way as you go" attitude—being willing to make mistakes and learn from them without hassling yourself unduly. That willingness to learn is probably what made you pick up this book.

You love your kids, you want to do your very best, and you are willing to learn. You have all the ingredients to be a fine parent!

Two Kinds of Love

WE LOVE OUR kids. But love is more than just a warm feeling—it involves some skill. Family therapists recognize that parents need to have two core qualities. I call these softlove and firmlove. Both of these kinds of love have to be activated in sufficient quantities in a parent's make-up, so that children receive the right ingredients to thrive. They are both available in you, but you may need some help to awaken them.

What Is Softlove?

Softlove is the ability to be relaxed, warm, and affectionate. It is the ability to stop your brain racing around, to trust your instincts, and to fend off the many pressures put on you from outside so that you can be there for your child. When you can relax and be yourself, your lovingness will just naturally arise.

You don't have to force softlove, but you do have to give it space to grow. Not everyone was raised with softlove, and so sometimes we find it hard to activate. If you had distant or aloof parents, then you may feel tense or uneasy, rather than relaxed and loving, when you are around babies or toddlers. As men and women rediscover softlove, many things will change for the better. Chapter 2 tells you how this is done.

What Is Firmlove?

Firmlove is the ability to be kind but firm with kids—to make clear rules and back them up, without getting angry, without being weak and giving in. It's the quality people speak of when they say, "That person has backbone."

Many people are confused about love because they think it is always warm and gooey. For instance, a father lends large amounts of money to his teenage daughter who "forgets" to pay him back. This isn't love—it's just "sogginess." Firmlove means saying, "Of course I love you. And you owe me $100. So no more loans till you pay me back!"

Firmlove is strength with a loving intention, as opposed to being cold and hard. Good parents are firm with little children often, because they love them. Often this relates to safety—"I love you, and that's why I won't let you run off down the street." Or respect for others—"In this house people don't hit each other."

Good parents are willing to be tough with their kids because they know this will help them to have happier lives.

Finding the Balance

No one gets it right every time. Giving softlove and firmlove to your kids is always a matter of finding your way, finding the balance as you go along. A parent who is kind and firm says things like—"No, you are not going out in the rain and cold. How about looking for something interesting to do in the kitchen?" They are aware of their child's need for activity—"I understand you are bored—I'll help you find something to do." But they are clear in their decision—"You have to stay indoors when it's wet."

Problems Are Your Cue to Adjust the Balance

The so-called problems that arise from time to time in every family are just your child's way of letting you know that the balance needs to change. For example, a little girl will get a tummyache because Mom and Dad have been too busy with the new baby. A boy will get into trouble at school to get more attention from his dad.

Sometimes you will have to develop new levels of either softlove or firmlove in yourself—more than you were ever given as a child—in order to help your child. That's why parenting is such a "stretching" time—it takes you beyond all your previous limitations. This has to be a good thing, but you will need support and encouragement. The chapters coming up will give you lots of this, with many real-life examples to draw on for inspiration.

Understanding Your Loving Style

LOTS OF parents have asked for a simple way to measure how they are doing—and how they can improve. This simple questionnaire can help you to understand the two kinds of love, and to make your parenthood a more positive experience. Circle the number that best reflects your answer.

SOFTLOVE QUESTIONS

1. I give my kids lots of hugs. I love to hold them and tell them how great they are.

   Not at all. 1   2   3   4   5 Very much.

2. I am a peaceful kind of person. I don't hurry. I can spend hours with my children just enjoying being together.

   Not at all. 1   2   3   4   5 Very much.

Now total the two scores above and enter your softlove total here.

Softlove Total _____

FIRMLOVE QUESTIONS

1. I can be clear, strong, and set rules, and get my children to follow them. The kids know when I mean business and nearly always obey.

   Not at all. 1   2   3   4   5 Very much.

2. I am calm and good-humored, so when I am being firm I don't often get really angry. I certainly never lash out at or hit my kids.

   Not at all. 1   2   3   4   5 Very much.

Now total the two scores above and enter your firmlove total here.

Firmlove Total _____

Now, enter your scores on the graph overleaf.

✦

Firmlove Score

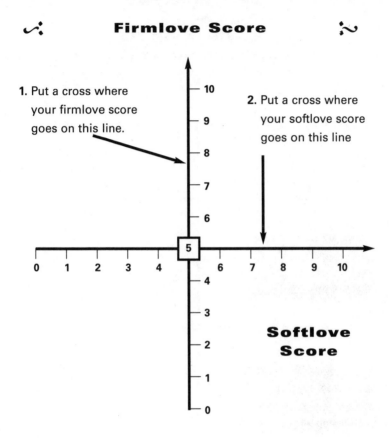

1. Put a cross where your firmlove score goes on this line.

2. Put a cross where your softlove score goes on this line

Softlove Score

3. Draw lines across and down from your two scores and mark where they meet. This is your loving style result.

4. Look on the next page for an explanation of your result.

⁀ Reading ∿ Your Scores

Roger is a strong, no-nonsense type of person who is well-organized. Maybe deep down he cares, but finds it hard to show this. So he is aloof and remote, and his kids may feel they are never quite good enough. He is often too busy to spend time with them. (Recently, though, he has started to change his ways.)

Penny is warm and very loving. She is also quite clear about discipline on the things that matter. Her kids know they have to follow certain guidelines and take on responsibilities. But they also feel safe and cared about. Everyone in this family has lots of fun, hugs, and laughter.

FIRM BUT COLD
Work on softlove skills described in chapter 2.

WARM AND STRONG
Great!

— 10
— 9
— 8
— 7
— 6
5
0 1 2 3 4   6 7 8 9 10
— 4
— 3
— 2
— 1
— 0

COLD AND NOT VERY STRONG
Work through chapters 2 and 3. Seek help from a caring counselor if you feel concerned about your parenting.

LOVING BUT NOT VERY FIRM
Work on firmlove skills described in chapter 3.

Agnes is very tense and distant. She may let her children get away with murder, and then loses it completely and lashes out at them. Then she feels sorry and goes back to being permissive again. (With the help of friends and a counselor she is learning to relax and love herself so she can love her children.)

Cheryl loves her kids and spends lots of time with them. In fact, she has no time for herself. The children walk all over her, and are very demanding. Cheryl is terribly tired from trying so hard, and yet can't seem to gain control. (She has started going to a parents' support group and is getting some hints on firmlove.)

The author wishes to apologize to any Agneses, Pennys, Rogers, or Cheryls who feel this is not them at all! No resemblance to any persons living, dead, or otherwise is intended.

~: **two** :~

Softlove

MAKING CONTACT WITH YOUR CHILD

ALL PARENTS LOVE THEIR CHILDREN.
THE BIG QUESTION IS—"WILL MY LOVE GET THROUGH?"

◆

It's DUSK, and the woods around the lake are silent, apart from a distant, lonely birdcall. In a cottage by the water, a man and a woman are making love. They begin slowly, taking their time, enjoying the anticipation and the gradual falling away of tensions and cares. They are getting to know each other afresh, though they have been partners for many years now. After a time, the energy and passion begins to rise, her laughter mingles with his urgency, and soon they are both crying out in pleasure. Afterward, there is a quiet resting and sleepy settling together of warm bodies. Later, inside the woman's body, as they both sleep, a sperm finds its way to the waiting, moon-like ovum, and a child's life begins.

LOVING THE LIFE INSIDE YOU

HOW DID YOU get to be a parent? You got pregnant—obviously! Did you want to get pregnant? Who knows? Your body certainly wanted to. To your conscious mind, though, becoming pregnant can be a shock. Even the most highly planned pregnancy (not to mention the most totally "accidental") brings this feeling. As you hold that little plastic test stick, you think, "Oh, my!" The roller-coaster ride has begun!

Being pregnant confronts you with a choice. You can reach out with love to this new life inside you, or you can pull back in fear and caution. As your child grows inside you, is born and grows up, you will again and again have the choice to harden your heart and pull back, or to soften your heart and respond with the quality we call softlove.

Softlove—the capacity for tenderness, generosity, and warmth—dwells inside every single person.

The softlove inside you may be strong like a fierce flame or it may stay like a tiny glowing spark, unnoticed, waiting to be kindled. Every new mother or father has this spark inside them. Researchers have found that when fathers are present at the birth, or get involved in the early care of babies, they become "engrossed" in the child—deeply interested and deeply satisfied—wanting to spend more of their time around the baby, and wanting to become skilled in the baby's care. This is true whether or not the baby is their own biological child. The key is being there early.

A mother's body, if she is able to sleep alongside her baby from the very first, and especially if she is helped to breast-feed, releases powerful hormones called prolactins that actually make her want to mother. These hormones relax her and slow her down, giving her deep pleasure in being with her little ones. They prime her body for awareness and vigilance around babies. Whenever you feel protective, drawn to anything small and furry, this is prolactin at work.

> *A note about breast-feeding. The evidence grows continually that breast-feeding provides nutrients and antibodies that make it far superior to artificial milk. Sometimes a mother has to bottle-feed through medical necessity, in which case it is important for her to bare her skin for the baby to feel while feeding. She should relax and make eye contact with her baby, and generally allow feeding time to be a time of intimacy. We believe that breast-feeding is an art—mothers sometimes need understanding help to breast-feed successfully and there are simple tips that can make all the difference. We recommend contacting the La Leche League. They can provide wonderful individual help to breast-feeding mothers, in almost every corner of the country. Or see their website: www.lalecheleague.org.*

So the loving feelings are inbuilt and waiting to be awakened. Sometimes this happens easily and smoothly. Sometimes it needs help.

WHEN YOU WERE A CHILD, DID YOU LEARN HOW TO LOVE?

IF YOU DIDN'T receive much love in your own childhood and babyhood, this can be one of the biggest barriers to letting your love flow—it may be that you didn't "learn to love." But it's never too late.

Our parents' generation cared about their children—but they didn't always show it, or say it very often. Many of today's parents were not raised with affection as babies and toddlers. In the "icy fifties," when medicine ruled birth and babyhood, it was considered "spoiling" to be kind to a child. Parents were instructed to leave their babies to cry, or were afraid to feed them unless the clock said they could, or worried they would corrupt their children by cuddling them. Even today some authors and pediatricians advise letting babies cry out their distress alone in their room. What a disaster!

Jean Liedloff, in an article in *Mothering* magazine, concludes that there are two basic feelings that all human beings need. These are to feel welcome, and to feel worthy. In the 1950s and '60s, parents were often very good at the mechanical side of parenting—feeding and clothing us and keeping us well. This was a pretty good start. But they often had trouble being warm or close, and in those days shame and blame were a big part of the discipline style. One could easily grow up feeling unwelcome, and unworthy to boot!

One man explained to us that in his teens and twenties he felt a strong need to be around older, kinder people, just to bathe in the feeling of being welcomed in, given a smile, being asked about his day. Gradually, through doing this, he filled in the gaps in his feelings of welcome. After a time, he also knew that people liked his company, asked his opinion, told him their problems—and that made him feel worthy. In the end he became a psychologist!

An old friend told us that when she was a girl, she used to feel very lonely and unloved. At midnight, when others were asleep, she would turn on the radio. The announcer on the late program had a deep, friendly voice. She would stay awake to hear him wish everyone "goodnight and God bless." Then she felt cared about and comforted, and slept soundly.

There were some pluses about childhood in "the old days." People tended to have lots of babies and lived close to their relatives, so older children, nieces, nephews, aunties, and grandmas all helped with the babies. You got lots of practice at being a parent before you became one. (Today a quarter of new parents have never even held a baby until the day they first hold their own. No wonder they are terrified.)

To avoid parenthood becoming a big struggle you must get extra help for yourself—learning to receive love, so you can love your baby well. This begins very early. Research has found that the presence of a support person at the birth—someone who loves and cares about the mother—dramatically reduces the incidence of caesareans, and of epidurals (and therefore forceps deliveries). Emotional care, in this case, of the mother, has real physical consequences.

Love is a real, tangible substance, and things go better when there is more love around. Once your baby is born, the best love people can give you is often practical: massage (for you), special meals, time, and care, as well as help to protect your privacy. All of these kinds of loving can help to awaken your own loving capacities.

In short, if you had a secure and loving childhood, then things are likely to go well with your kids. But even if you didn't—and many of us didn't—then you can still turn things around for yourself and your children.

Healing a Mother Helps a Son

*E*SME, **THIRTY-EIGHT**, had a difficult relationship with her teenage son. In fact, he was very depressed and possibly suicidal. We talked about how she and he got along. It was clear that almost every conversation they had involved her criticizing him. On the inside she cared, but on the outside she was cool and stiff, and very unhappy with herself. As she felt safer with me, Esme confided that she rarely if ever hugged her son or touched him in an affectionate way. The very idea of touching him made her uncomfortable.

Emotional coolness on a mother's part is known to be a danger sign for suicide in teenage boys, especially if the father is also ineffectual or distant. So we made closeness our first goal. With encouragement, Esme began to reach out more. She practiced casually putting a hand on her son's shoulder as she gave him his dinner, and giving him small compliments on his hair or clothes. After a week or two she moved up to giving him a brief hug when he left for school.

Esme found it hard to do these things, but she persisted. Then, one day in a self-development course she was attending, she was listening to someone in the group talking about their painful childhood. Suddenly she found she was shaking and shivering, and soon she was sobbing out loud. She was remembering being sexually assaulted by her father when she was about four. (Fortunately, her mother had left her father shortly after that.)

Esme had not so much forgotten these incidents as played down their importance to herself. Here was the reason why she found touch and affection difficult.

Through talking little by little in the group about her experiences, Esme learned to let others care for her, and she rapidly became a more outgoing person. All these qualities had been latent inside her, but were hidden by the fear of a little four-year-old girl whose trust had been betrayed. So helping her son turned into helping herself too.

✦

THE POWER OF TOUCH

WHEN YOU READ the story of Esme and her son, did it surprise you that touch and affection could make the difference between a youngster wanting to live and wanting to die? Can touch really be that important?

On the surface, one wouldn't think that teenagers would be so concerned about their parents' affection. But a teenager was once a baby. And if they were not cuddled and stroked back then, it was a serious matter indeed.

Starved of affection, a little baby can literally die of loneliness. When a premature baby is stroked, growth hormones are produced. It's as if a baby decides life is worth living. When we receive loving touch our immune system fires up and resists infection much more readily. Hemoglobin (iron-carrying) levels in the blood increase dramatically.

Touch is an "essential vitamin" for all mammals. When babies are born prematurely, they are often kept in incubators for many weeks. It has been discovered recently that if these babies are regularly stroked by their mother (or another loving person) reaching into the crib and caressing their little bodies gently, they will gain weight 75 percent faster than other babies who are not given this stroking. They are discharged weeks earlier, and save the hospital thousands of dollars.

Find as Many Ways to Touch as You Can

There are many ways to show affection to small children—massage, stroking, patting, tickling, caressing, carrying, rocking, cuddling, brushing their hair, holding hands, giving rides, swinging, jiggling. Each conveys a different version of the same message—you are loved, you are welcome, you are worthy.

Sometimes older children go through a non-touch phase where they are establishing some independence. An experienced mother of teenagers told us that you have to still "keep your arms open," because the time will come when they want to be hugged again.

Early problems and deprivations can often be healed later by gradually building up affection, as a child learns to trust. With sufficient time and care, fostered and adopted babies can overcome a difficult beginning. I have often seen and worked with adults who are healing babyhood neglect, and doing it successfully. But it is so much better to get it right the first time.

THE POWER OF PRAISE

AS KIDS GET older, there are even more ways to make our love known to them. The most obvious way is with words. We shape their personality—by saying, "You are beautiful, you are lots of fun, you are good to be around." Kids become what we tell them they are.

Children need two kinds of telling. One kind is unconditional praise—this means that we let them know—"I love you because you are you." They don't have to earn this love, and they can't ever lose it. Imagine how good this feels—to be unconditionally loved, just because you exist.

The second kind is conditional praise. This means that we tell them, "I appreciate your actions." For instance, we might say, "I like the way you entertained your baby sister when the phone rang," or "Gee, I like your drawings," or "You sing beautifully," and so on.

It's okay to tell kids what you don't like as well—as long as you don't call them names. "You didn't pick up your clothes very well—I can still see eight T-shirts and seventeen socks on the floor" is fine. "You lazy little slob" is not so good.

Sometimes parents have to learn to see the positives before they can point them out. The power of our attention is a very powerful influence on our children. A good way to think of it is: "What you focus on with kids is what you get." Some families focus on illness, for example, and always have sick kids. Some focus on complaining (while trying to make everyone happy), and always have grumpy kids. If you look for negatives and always point these out (which some fathers are especially prone to doing), then the negatives will increase. If you let your children know that you notice when they act well, and comment on what they do that is great, then they will act great more of the time!

Quality of the Week

*H*ERE IS an exercise to try.

1. Choose the three qualities you most want your child to have (it could be anything—kindness to others, patience, gentleness, perseverance, cooperation, independence, creativity).
2. Take one of these qualities as your goal for this week.
3. Take note of every time your child shows this quality.

Comment sometimes, other times just simply notice. Make no negative comments at all. By the end of the week, you can be sure this quality will be on the increase. Then move on to another. You can also let your child choose a quality, and notice it together through the week. Point out only when the child does show the quality.

✦

TIME

THERE IS ONE essential ingredient for softlove—that is, being there; or in other words, having time. However much you tell your children you love them, if you are not around enough, then your words will be a lie. With kids it's what you do, not what you say, that counts.

Lots of fathers today leave for work at 7:30 A.M. and return at 7:30 P.M. or later. These fathers are not likely to be successful as parents, or if they are, will only be so by making superhuman efforts on vacations and weekends. It isn't always their fault—the workplace is not yet a parent-friendly place. In the Stone Age, parents would often have to face a tiger or woolly mammoth to save their children. In the computer age, we might have to tell our boss to "buzz off!"—equally dangerous.

It's not just dads—lots of mothers too are being conned by the comforting but largely false concept of "quality time." (To my shame, I went along with this idea in my earlier work.) You can't have quality time with children "to order," by schedule, on the dot. Relationships are a delicate business. If a woman has a husband who suddenly puts down the newspaper or turns off the TV at 10:30 at night and gets all amorous after ignoring her all evening, she'll know the feeling that kids get when a parent tries to spend "quality time!"

Certainly it's important to have special times. One easy and very powerful step to take is to sit down for a meal together each day, and switch off the TV or radio. It can be dinner, or even breakfast. Too few families eat together, yet it can be one perfect way to reconnect.

To a large degree, kids decide what they are worth based on what they are worth to you, and based on your enjoyment of their company. Imagine how good it feels to a baby or toddler to know that you value them more highly than almost anything else. As babies and toddlers, they should feel this way—not that they are "the boss," but that their needs really count. This need reduces as they get older, but is still operating well into their teens.

INCREASING YOUR CAPACITY FOR LOVE

WHAT IS THE quickest way to increase the love and positivity available in your family? You can start by learning a simple skill that all loving people have, often without knowing it. This is the knack of living in "present time."

Present time is where children live. To them, the future is impossibly far off. Kids live for today!

You were like this once. Can you remember when you were little, and a day seemed like a really long time? When two months off from school at the start of the summer seemed like forever?

An adult who can live in the now (at least some of the time) will be an instant hit with children. Old people sometimes have this ability because they've stopped rushing. Most parents (the people who most need to be) are hardly ever in present time. (As a young parent, I had a bad case of this. Whenever I was with my children, my mind would be somewhere else. My toddler son would give me a whack to bring me back to attention.)

Many people seem to have lost the knack of just being—especially if they live in cities, away from the rhythms of nature. Or worse still, they think they are "wasting time" or "not achieving" if a day just drifts by. Yet if you want to get through to your kids, whether to show them your love, or to give them effective discipline, then you have to get yourself back into present time. Here is how to do just that.

Getting Your Brain to Come Home

Most of the trouble we have in life comes from having a brain. Not just any brain, but a human brain—horribly prone to worries and abstractions that no dog, cat, or bird would ever waste a second on. (A mother once commented at one of my seminars, "I worry if my children will ever get a job." I asked how old her kids were and she said, "Oh, I don't have kids yet!" She'd come along to my talk as a preparation for parenthood! Half of me thought, "Great!" and half of me thought, "This gal should be bowling!")

Our brain can make us miserable because it is always racing off out of control. So we miss out on what is happening right in front of us. There are three ways your brain "races off."

1. **Dragging around in the past.** Recalling the past can be very pleasant, but mostly people go into the past to rehash old regrets (what they missed out on), old guilts (what they shouldn't have done but did!) and old resentments (what others didn't do but should have).

   Going over the past, without changing any of it or having any new thoughts, is often a complete waste of time. Yet it probably occupies half of all human mental activity!

2. **Racing ahead to the future.** The future can also be a wonderful place to dream about, but most people just worry about what can go wrong. They use the future to practice "worst-case scenarios" (a beautiful phrase!). Rent the video *Parenthood*, and watch the baseball scene for a brilliant example of this.

The trouble with fearing the worst is that it either paralyzes you, or else you react to things in an exaggerated way. You overlook the positive because it doesn't fit your plan of disaster. You miss the beauty of the roses because you are imagining yourself catching tetanus from the thorns.

3. **Wishing you were somewhere else (or thinking you should be).** Lots of people make themselves miserable by wishing they had made the other decision—taken that job, taken that class, married the other guy or girl, lived in that other town, not had this baby. They are in one place, but yearn for another. Everyone does this at times, but sensible people use the energy to make changes, plan a vacation, or organize the future to more resemble the dreams they have. Others, though, just yearn. If only . . . aah, then I would be happy.

While we are busy racing off in our minds, we are making ourselves miserable, and we are missing out on our children.

HAPPINESS, LIKE A CHILD, DWELLS IN THE PRESENT

IN CASE YOU hadn't noticed by now, many of the best times in life just happen. Happiness often doesn't come according to plan. (Sometimes it does—the planned vacation or outing, a family occasion, a well-deserved trip to a restaurant or the movies.) But for every planned happiness there are ten accidental ones that will only happen if you allow them to—if you have enough time to appreciate them. Happiness is like a butterfly, waiting for you to stand still so it can land on your shoulder.

Magic Moments

LIFE DELIVERS us pearls of happiness when we least expect them. (New-car commercials on TV try to capture these moments.)

You know the kind of thing—you're in a field or park with your children trying to fly a kite. It's cloudy. At first, the kite won't fly, then suddenly—it's up! The kids are running toward you with the kite trailing behind. An eagle soars overhead. The sun is out suddenly and shining through their hair like golden haloes. Everything goes into slow motion, and are those violins you hear? Your partner smiles at you adoringly and you are suddenly and absolutely "blissed out." You wouldn't be anywhere else for a million dollars!

✦

Children store up these moments in their memory banks. At quiet times, or on long car trips, your kids will play "Remember when . . . ?" recalling in detail the good times they had at that place and this. It builds their sense of belonging and their optimism for the future. Can you remember the really magical moments in your own childhood? I can remember a day at a soccer match with my dad, being kept warm inside his long overcoat. I can remember being held by my mother on the toilet when I was a toddler. She sat on the laundry basket opposite me, and I leaned onto her lap. Perhaps she was worried I would fall in. Whatever the reason, it felt nice. I remember making it last!

∿ Happy Endings—Every Day! ∿

ONE FAMILY we know has a five-year-old son and a two-year-old daughter. Each night, when they go to bed, these kids have a special ritual. Instead of reading a story, their mom or dad recounts the events of the day.

At the end of this story, they tell their child what was the very best part of the day for them. Then they ask their child, "What was the best part of your day?" and listen carefully to what they have to say. Then they kiss goodnight.

It's a beautiful way to end the day, and a very powerful programming of energy toward the positive.

Madness Runs in Families

FAMILY LIFE these days often resembles organized madness. Parents rise before 6:00 A.M., gulp down some food, rush children to before-school care, then to school, which takes them to after-school care. They pick them up after work, go home, make them a snack, have "quality time" (ho, ho!), do housework or office work brought home, and then collapse asleep after midnight.

Families today often own houses that require both adults working for thirty years to pay off. Some parents spend a quarter of their waking time sitting in a vehicle. Fathers often have to work nights to pay private school fees for children who hate school anyway, and have low self-esteem and drug problems because their fathers are never home. Marriages collapse from neglect and fatigue, but both partners blame "communication problems." Both partners get more quality communication with the lady behind the counter at the local coffee shop! The American family seems to be dying of stress.

✦

BEING "GROUNDED" —A TECHNIQUE FOR CALMING DOWN

GROUNDING IS A powerful and simple way of getting your mind to settle down and be focused on the here and now. You can do grounding anywhere—driving a car, doing the dishes, walking down the corridor, making love. Here is how it is done.

Why not try this right now, as you read. Start by noticing your own body's "inside sensations"—how your muscles feel, how your insides feel. Just notice these inner sensations, however slight. Focus on the inner sensations in your body, however vague they might be. Then start to notice what you are touching—your hands on this book (are your shoulders relaxed?), the chair pressing your back, the feel of your clothes on your skin. Just notice and intensify the sensations that are already there.

After a time, shift your focus to the outside. Look around you, smell and listen to what is around you. Become intensely aware of your surroundings. Literally "come to your senses."

You will notice the three distinct layers of experience: your insides (the sensations inside your body)—are you energetic, tired, relaxed, do you need to shift your position? your edges— what you are touching, your hands on this book, the air on your face; your environment—what is going on around you, what sounds, what colors, what action is around you?

As you notice these three zones of awareness without expecting or judging anything, you will become aware of several effects.

Your mind will slow down.

You will intensify the present moment—the beauty of it, the richness of it.

Your body signals will come through more strongly, telling you there is something that needs to be done—stretch your legs, go for a pee, get something to eat! And so on.

At times, we are all troubled by an overactive mind. The best way to calm your mind is to give it something to attend to, something that is real and present. If you are driving a car, notice the feel of the steering wheel; if you are stacking the dishwasher, the feel of the dishes; if you are sitting with your child, the touch and temperature of his or her body against yours.

Unlike relaxation, grounding can be done anywhere in a matter of seconds. Using grounding takes practice and mindfulness, but it is as natural as breathing. Do it, and it will be totally reliable in improving your state of mind. Little children are usually already grounded. People who are very natural, rhythmic, and down to earth are grounded and you can learn to be the same by just being around them. As you learn to be grounded more of the time, you will be less interested in being any other way. You will notice when you are getting too speedy or agitated, or depressed and stuck in your thoughts. You will be able to bring yourself smoothly back to the pleasures of the here and now.

SELF-TIME—WHAT EVERY PARENT NEEDS

YOU CAN'T GIVE love if you don't have a clear sense of self. And a sense of self comes only when you give yourself space to be. Every day, you must keep some time just for yourself.

Some people get up early, or stay up late when everyone else has gone to bed, to get this time. Others make a deal with their partner to provide some self-time for each other.

Self-time is even more important than couple-time, because you cannot connect with your partner until you have re-established a sense of self. Once you are happy in yourself, you will feel like being close to another person, but not usually until then.

Self-time doesn't mean doing housework, though sometimes a big cleanup while the kids are being looked after can be very satisfying. It could mean time with friends. Watching TV doesn't do it well—you lose yourself rather than find yourself. Writing works very well—letters or a journal. Praying or meditation is good if you have a spiritual dimension in your life. Reading is pretty good. Lie in the bath with a glass of wine and a magazine! Head off to the country, go into the garden, walk the dog. Everyone has their preferred way of having self-time. The important thing is to do it and to schedule it regularly.

The Tree of (Family) Life

You grow a family like you grow a tree. The roots are your own childhood and how you care for yourself. The trunk is your marriage or partnership, and your commitment to your kids. The branches are your actions based on choices you make every day. Your kids are the flowers and the fruit.

We live in as natural a way as possible, try to eat clean food, and work to make our world and neighborhood better and safer places.

We cultivate good friendships. Relationships with grandparents, neighbors, cousins, and special friends provide a support nework of people I can confide in.

We dance around and play music and sing.

I am firm about my kids' behavior, especially about respect for each others' rights and feelings.

I protect my kids from exposure to dangerous people and violent or cheap media.

I take steps to control how much my job intrudes on my family and my life.

I hug my kids, and laugh and play with them often.

I really like my children and enjoy spending time with them. They make me feel good (most of the time).

I work on my marriage and set aside time to get to know my partner. I do this for myself, for my partner, and for my children.

I'd rather be with my kids and be poor than have money but no time to spend with them.

I care for myself, and have time just to be me.

People were kind to me when I was young and I enjoy passing that on to the children of today.

I had a tough time as a kid, so I know it's important to 'water and feed the roots'. This will help me to do good things and to get good things and good care for myself.

LETTING KIDS BE KIDS

Once, long ago, I worked in a high school with dropout children. One day during recess time, a group of my twelve-year-olds disappeared behind a huge stack of damaged furniture and I could hear giggles and shuffling sounds from deep in the heap. I suspected "evildoing" and crawled in to investigate. To my embarrassment, they were sharing their lunches in a kind of clubhouse! They invited me to join them, but I just grinned and crawled ashamedly outside to the noisy world. I'd forgotten these were really just children, needing to play.

Perhaps the most serious and insidious harm that has been done to children in the last twenty years has been caused by the way we have taken away their childhood. There are several ways that this happens.

1. **A media bombardment.** Horror, fear, grief, and pain are compressed daily into our media news and our entertainment. TV has a little screen, so it has to have a big shock to hold our attention. The media blasts the same messages at toddlers as it does at sixty-year-olds. We heap our children with needless negativity that is not relevant to their lives and that they are in no way equipped to deal with.

2. **An overscheduled life.** Many families I know of spend evenings and weekends shuffling children to a range of sports, music, culture, and supplementary learning venues. When all these "extras" are combined with homework pressures, the average child has very little time just to be a child. We have the most overscheduled generation that ever existed. A solution to this might be a simple rule—one child, one activity.

3. **A competitive neurosis.** Partly fueling the second point is the feeling, easily caught by children, that life is a desperate race. So school takes on an anxious, performance-laden aura, even from kindergarten. Instead of playing around, children join a competitive, organized, often expensive sport. Seven-year-olds are comparing their scores, worrying about their performances, praying they will make the team. This is madness.
4. **Overworked parents.** Since we are so busy providing all these goodies, we have little time or energy to make contact. We become tense, snappy, and poor confidantes to our children. Feeling guilty, we provide more possessions and experiences, and then have to work harder still to pay for them.
5. **An unsafe world.** Whereas once children roamed the neighborhoods of fifties America, barely seen from breakfast till dinner, we now have to guard them carefully and protect them from traffic, strangers, and crime.

We need a re-greening of childhood—a conservationist approach. We have to conserve the rare, natural, and wild part of our children. This is an active process—cutting out and fencing off needless pressures and invasions. We have to "de-pollute" our children's lives.

Some Possible Tips

+ Have lots of time, space, and materials for simple play. Plastic toys are cheap and clean, but mud and scrap paper, clay and water are the best toys. They give absolutely free rein to the child's own inclinations and imagination.
+ Create healthy boredom—kids used to being entertained by computer screens, videos, or schedules of "educational" activity will take a little while to switch over to

self-initiated play. You may have to resist "I'm bored" for a time until they begin self-starting.

+ Play is valuable in itself. Psychologists are discovering that this is the way children make sense of their world, act out concerns, overcome fears, and learn to relate to others. Play is the source of all creativity and inventiveness. The great musicians, scientists, lovers, artists, and even managers are the ones who have preserved the ability to play with their ideas and their work.

+ You can play, too—adults in crisis or transition often find healing in creativity, music, natural places, movement, and the outdoors.

+ Stop watching the evening news. Don't have a TV set running in the house—choose programs and watch them, then turn the TV off. Give kids an hour a day and let them select what they will watch.

+ Consider your whole lifestyle in this question. Do you really like where you live, how you live, and the work that you do? Are there alternatives that would make your life more joyful, simpler, and yet still stimulating and rich? Perhaps we are living at a time when the whole world needs to "wind down." Children give you a good reason to do this.

Sometimes the arrival of babies in our lives kicks us into a frenzy of overactivity—renovating, working overtime to save for school fees, trying to provide what we think they need. When all the time what they really need is us!

My work with families in distress has given me an extra spur to not waste my life with busyness—in one simple and trenchant way. Sometimes children die—and if we have missed out on the present while working for the future, then we will feel very bad indeed.

The best thing you can do for your children is enjoy them.

ᴗ Special Discovery—New ᴗ Vitamins Children Need

*W*E ALL know about the vitamins A to K, which we need in our daily diet to thrive and grow. It is rumored that scientists have recently discovered some more vitamins that are just as essential. Here they are.

Vitamin M—for music. Naturally occurring in young parents, can be added to family's diet immediately. Put on great music and dance with the kids in your living room—often. Pick them up if they are too small, and dance around with them. Sing in the car, collect favorite tapes. Have some simple instruments around. If you take your kids to music lessons, make sure they are satisfying, or at least good fun, for your child.

Endangered by constant radio or TV noise—child learns not to hear.

Vitamin P—for poetry. Teach little chants and rhymes to toddlers. Older kids can recite and perform favorite short poems at family gatherings. Listen to stories and poetry on tape to enjoy the spoken voice. Fred Hollows's "Man from Snowy River" and similar recordings are magical for older kids.

Vitamin N—for nature. Make chances for your children to experience total nonhuman environments. For little kids, a backyard will do—lots of wild insects and creepy-crawlies, bird-attracting shrubs and trees. But whenever you can, get into the woods, and go to the beach. Watch sunsets. Camp out. Closely related to Vitamin S for spirituality, sometimes available at churches, temples, mosques, and the like.

Endangered by computer games, living in cities, too many theme parks, and thinking that pleasure is something you buy.

Vitamin F—for fun. Available anywhere. Rubs off from children onto adults, and back again. Most common vitamin in the universe. Not naturally present in the workplace, but can be smuggled in.

Endangered by wearing a watch.

Vitamin H—for hope. Hope is naturally occurring. You just have to make sure it isn't removed by exposure to toxins. Avoid watching the news or viewing the world through newspapers. Don't indulge in gloom-mongering around kids—especially teenagers. Join something that makes a difference—Greenpeace, Wilderness Society, Community Aid Abroad "Aware" program—whose publications are incredibly positive. Research has shown that kids with even slightly activist parents are more mentally healthy, have a more positive view of the world and the future, and do more about it.

✦

‿: **three** :‿

Firmlove

THE SECRET OF WELL-BEHAVED CHILDREN

◆

It's A SIGN of the times that people are even using the word *discipline* again. For those of us who grew up in the sixties, this is an amazing turnaround. For a while there, the only place you saw the word *discipline* being used was in some very weird sites on the Internet.

But sure enough, as you leaf through family magazines and scan the bookshelves, discipline is back on the agenda. And not a moment too soon. When most modern houses include a room called a parents' retreat, then it's clearly time to act. Let's reclaim the house!

WHY DISCIPLINE?

UH-OH! YOU have just spotted them coming up the driveway. Your best friend with her child—the toddler from hell. The kid who puts jam on your sofa, writes on the curtains, and frightens pit bull terriers. Should you answer the door? Is there time to hide?

Discipline is a funny thing—you notice it most when it isn't there. Everyone knows someone with a completely out-of-control child, and many of us have one of our own! Getting cooperation is a problem at times for almost every parent. Most parents in the U.S. today are confused about discipline.

A small number of parents, on the other hand, seem to have it all sorted out. What is their secret? These parents call their toddler to "come along now" and the toddler actually comes! You visit their house and your mouth hangs open. Their ten-year-old makes a snack for the family. Their teenagers phone to say they'll be home early. And these kids are not frightened mice—they're happy, optimistic, and relaxed. How do these parents do it?

We all long to have well-disciplined kids for one simple reason—it makes life go more smoothly. Giving in to kids doesn't make life easier. Parents who are reluctant to set boundaries find

that their kids just get worse. Without clear rules, you and your child may spend the whole day bickering, and everyone feels bad at the end of it. Whereas if you have a discipline method that works quickly, problems are soon solved and you can get on with being happy.

There is more to it, though. We don't discipline kids just for our own sakes—just to have "law and order." After all, if you want an orderly life, you don't have kids. The real purpose of discipline is to teach children to operate happily and easily in the world.

Without some parental firmness, children don't develop inner controls, and they just keep on acting like two-year-olds, even when they are five, fifteen, twenty-five. Without inner discipline, a child's life is a mess. Parents who let children do as they like will severely disable them for living in the real world. These kids may end up unhappy, unemployed, unmarried, lonely, angry, and perhaps even in jail. A child who has been taught good self-discipline, on the other hand, learns how to negotiate the world and stay out of trouble, and so is really free.

Discipline is about getting along with yourself and with other people. After love, there is nothing more important you can give them than discipline. But not the kind of discipline that has often been implied by that word.

The approach to discipline we recommend is called firmlove—it is intervening out of love for the child. A parent using firmlove says, "I love you, and that's why I will stop you behaving like this." They combine love and firmness. They never hit, they never harm, they never blame. But they are firm.

"Stand and Think" and "Dealing"

By now, you may be asking—"What is this miraculous method of getting cooperation?" It's a good time to explain. Firmlove rests on two main techniques—the first is called "stand and think" and the second is called "dealing." These methods are used from toddlerhood onward, modified and developed as your child grows, and adaptable into adolescence and adulthood. In fact, the ability to "stand and think" and "deal" will become inner resources throughout your child's adult life, helping them to be mature, reflective, and wise in all their dealings.

Let's find out how it's done.

⌒ Lucy Meets Her Match ↜

TWENTY-MONTH-OLD Lucy is playing with the power cords at the back of the stereo. She isn't doing this quietly or sneakily—she is in full view of her mother and father, who are deep in conversation. Her mother sees her and calls out, "Lucy, hands off those power cords. Come away and play with your toys."

Lucy doesn't even budge. Her mother stands up and goes over to her—"Lucy, hands off the power cords, come over here." Lucy looks up and gives the famous "What are you going to do about it?" look. Her mother gives it one more try—"Come away from the power cords!" Lucy turns back to rewiring the stereo, muttering "No, no, no!" under her breath.

Up until today, Lucy has never done anything this naughty. She has always been able to be diverted or negotiated away from trouble. Today, though, is her first real discipline experience. She is inviting her parents to struggle with her because this is what she needs.

It's time for action. Lucy's mother moves in briskly, grabs Lucy around the waist from behind with both hands, lifts her clear and takes her to the other side of the room where there is an empty corner (every playroom should have an empty corner). Lucy does not welcome this attention. She screams, yells, hits out, and flails (which is why her mom is holding her from behind!). Her mom continues to hold her firmly, safely, and tells her, "When you are ready to calm down, you can come out."

Lucy goes through many "moves" that may be familiar to you—spitting, trying to bite, attempting to vomit her dinner up. Other children may hold their breath, call you names, and so on. Lucy has never been smacked and is not at all afraid. In fact, she is furious. How dare anyone interfere with her impulses! She looks to her father, who is standing back across the room. "Daddy, helpa me!" Her father moves in and helps to hold her. He repeats what her mother has been telling her, in a calm, reassuring tone: "You must stay away from power cords, Lucy." After what seems like ten minutes, but is actually about one minute, Lucy stops fighting and quiets down. Her mother has been saying to her softly the whole time,

"When you are ready to calm down, you can come out."
She now asks Lucy straight out, "Now, are you going to
stay away from the power cords?" "Yeth!"

Both parents stand back. "Good girl," they say, and
watch to see what she will do. Lucy looks at the power
cords. She looks at her parents. She looks at her toys on
the other side of the room. Then she heads over to the
toys. And her mom and dad give a big sigh of relief and
sit back down. In the weeks that follow, Lucy will try
"plugging in the power cords" once more, and stop
when spoken to.

She will be in and out of the "thinking spot" many
times before she is five years old—for all kinds of reasons. By age two and a half she will usually go there
when told to, and stand quietly and think over what she
needs to learn. By five, she will have learned to think, to
consider her actions, to account for the feelings of others,
and still be a happy, spontaneous, and easygoing child.

No Hurt, No Blame, No Fear

FOR LITTLE LUCY, getting carried off to "stand and think" was a surprise, but only her pride was dented—and only for a matter of minutes. With little children, we sometimes have to be physical, although always safe and never scary. By carrying a screaming toddler away from a supermarket when they want to stay, restraining them from pouring a soft drink into a sleeping dog's ears, breaking up a melee at the play group—we have to physically let them know "that's not OK!" With a toddler, we have to match words with actions. Move calmly without hurting (even when you are angry). In fact, it's best to act early, long before you lose your cool. If you feel too stirred up, then forget the dealing, and just put them in their room till you cool down.

Soon you will be able to simply tell your child to go to a chosen spot in the room, to "stand and think." Your child will do so, knowing there is no option, but also knowing that it won't take long and isn't a big issue or a punishment—just the way forward through a problem. The emphasis is on the child finding a solution that is acceptable.

Is It Naughtiness or Is It Just Energy?

YOU ONLY have to look at the human body to realize it is made for movement.

In his beautiful book *The Songlines,* Bruce Chatwin reports that Bushmen and -women in the Kalahari carry their babies for 2,500 miles on average before the little ones can walk by themselves.

Our bodies were designed to range over many miles each day. So adults or children will feel restive and bored just staying still. Worse still, playing a computer game or watching exciting TV will make kids feel quite twitchy— since these activities create adrenaline with nothing to expend it on. Kids have to get outside and get lots of whole-body exercise every day.

Occupational therapist Kerry Anne Brown believes that many later skills, like reading, handwriting, posture, and general coordination, depend on children running, climbing, bouncing, catching, and expending huge amounts of energy in the early years of school. These early activities help organize the brain and build muscles to assist in the development of smaller movements, like pen holding, later on. Even carrying little babies in slings and backpacks really helps—as do all those roughhouse games that dads tend to play with little ones on the play-room floor.

A trampoline is a great investment, and any kind of climbing and swinging devices that are safe and well designed are worth their weight in gold.

Parks are also a big plus. Lobby your city council to provide plenty of playgrounds in warm, sheltered spots, with shade from the sun and seats for adults. They should be near houses, not off in unsafe areas where young moms feel exposed. They should be well fenced, so you can read a magazine and not worry that your kids can wander off. Good clean toilet facilities would help.

When you are going up the wall, go to a park. I have spent many Saturdays traveling from playground to playground which, with occasional snacks and sand-wiches, kept my kids totally (and cheaply) satisfied!

◆

BEYOND THE OLD METHODS

THERE HAVE BEEN three main approaches to discipline over the past hundred years. Traditionally, people used hitting and hurting to frighten kids into behaving. Later, as hitting fell from favor, parents instead used blame and guilt to shame children into behaving. In recent times, people have used isolation methods, such as "time-out." As we know from sending adults to prison, isolating people often doesn't teach them much. So very little changes.

Firmlove goes beyond any of these, recognizing that discipline is about getting involved and teaching. Discipline is not about punishment. One of the great things about firmlove—using "stand and think" and learning to "deal"—is that you will never need to smack or hit your kids. Your children—and perhaps one day all children—can grow up without fearing their parents in any way. Can you imagine how good that would feel?

Firmlove means confronting children, certainly, and letting them handle some discomfort, but never inflicting pain. The aim of firmlove is simply to help children find better ways.

Let's look at another instance.

HOW TO USE THE "STAND AND THINK" AND "DEALING" METHODS

1. Preparation. Ask yourself, "What's wrong here? What do I want them to do to fix it?" In other words, have a clear goal before you start.
2. Learning to stand and think is a skill in itself. With a young toddler, it is enough to take them to the spot you have decided on, and then stand back a little. Tell them, "You have to stay there until you are ready to agree. You

can come out when you've calmed down," or if you are holding them, "I'll let you go when you calm down." At this age, as soon as they show signs of relenting, or mumble a few words of apology, let them out. Make it easy for them to get it right. For example, if they are throwing a toy at the wall and you want them to put it in a box, bring the box close.

3. As children get older (two or three plus), the conversation they have with you gets more important. Remember, they have to convince you that things are going to be different. They have to "talk their way out" and convince you they can act differently. Another good name for this is "dealing." They are learning to "deal."

   Tell them their task—"Stand there and think about what you did to get into this trouble. As soon as you've figured it out, I'll come and we'll talk about it."

   Your manner and voice should not be angry or scary, but firm and positive—you love them and are encouraging them to get it right.

   If you are jittery, stressed, or furious, don't attempt to do "stand and think." Manage the situation some other way, such as using a time-out. Wait till you are calmer, or until the problem recurs, to talk it over with them. Use "stand and think" when you have the time and motivation to get them over this particular hurdle and learning a better way.

   If you feel terribly angry at your child, as if you might start to hit them, make sure your child is safe, and go out of the room, or into the yard, and cool off. If it happens a few days in a row, seek help. Tell a friend, or your doctor, or a counselor. Call a parent help line for suggestions about what is the best help in your area. It's normal to need lots of support with a difficult toddler, and seeking help isn't something to be ashamed of.

4. The dealing conversation. Ask them:
   a) "What did you do?" Owning up to one's actions is important.
   b) "What were you feeling or needing?"
   c) "What should you have done to meet your needs?" Do they know a better way?

   Have you discussed this before? Perhaps you will need to teach them. For example, maybe they could join in a game others are playing, use a timer to share a toy fairly, put toys where a baby won't wreck them.

   d) "What are you going to do in the future?" Get a commitment.
   e) "Show me." Go ahead and do it right now—get it right this time.
5. Aim for a happy ending. The beauty of "dealing" properly like this is that the issue is resolved. You invest

some time right now, and the problem need never recur (well, maybe once or twice). You'll know that this was successful because you end up feeling better, and your child feels better. Everyone is redeemed.

A WHOLE NEW APPROACH

THIS IS A very different form of discipline from those that have been used in the past. When we look back to our childhoods, many of us associate discipline with feeling bad. The history of parenting since the industrial revolution has often been one of cruelty and distress for children. Many parents in the old days had little skill, and often simply repeated what was done to them (even though they hated it at the time).

Once discipline is understood properly there is no need for hurt, shame, or fear. The methods of firmlove are part of a breakthrough that is spreading all over the world. Good parents have intuitively found these approaches throughout history, but they have rarely been spelled out in a way that can be learned.

Firmlove methods are respectful of children, are nonviolent, and yet clearly place parents in charge. We believe these methods can bring about a revolution in child rearing, making it easier and much more enjoyable to produce young adults who are strong, loving, and safe.

THE THREE TRICKS OF GETTING COOPERATION

MANY CONFRONTATIONS CAN be prevented. If you think ahead, you can often prevent situations from reaching confrontation level. To begin with you may need to use "stand and think" quite a few times a day with little children. Soon, though, they learn to act on an early warning, or a count of "one, two, three." A lot of the time, experienced parents find they can prevent problems by some forethought, and divert them when they do happen, so that confrontations are kept to a manageable minimum. This means that as children get to age three or four, you can save your firmlove skills (and your energy) for the times once or twice a day when some important lesson needs to be addressed. Here are some ways to avoid problems—some of the time.

Prevention

A lot of kid trouble arises out of stress, fatigue, and hunger.

Make sure you and your child have a good meal before going out, and stop for snacks regularly. Avoid really high sugar foods, except as an occasional treat or after eating a meal. Most kids get zippy and harder to manage after a big sugar "hit."

Time your activities and leave out nonessentials, so that you are not pressured and forced to race the clock. While raising toddlers, it's important to simplify your life. Little things suddenly take a lot longer to do, so do yourself a favor and allow for this.

Make your day ritualized and pleasantly rhythmic, so that kids get used to the routine. When getting ready for school or kindergarten, tell your kids to dress themselves first, before they eat breakfast. This avoids delays and hassles about dressing—hungry kids dress quickly without making a fuss. (Getting them to eat a good breakfast is simple—just give them a slightly smaller dinner the night before. They will wake up ravenous!)

Make time at home happy. Have a fun time doing ordinary things—play fun music while doing the housework. Slow down your expectations of perfection. Be a happy slob. You only have kids full-time for five years, and half-time for about ten years more. Why not enjoy it?

Sometimes little children who are restless just need more exercise—the modern world of small yards, car seat belts, long drives, and a dangerous environment, is two-thirds of the problem. Sandpits, waterplay, and room to run and climb make a huge difference. Kids need to run off huge amounts of energy, like puppies, and often some outdoor time is all they need to be much more settled and peaceful.

Diversion

Often trouble can be avoided by finding a better way, striking a bargain, even bribery—"I'll buy you some chips at the store, but you'll have to help me and get into your car seat." A child fighting another over a toy can be offered a longer turn if they go second. Kids can learn to use a timer, to take turns, to play in such a way that all can participate. Sometimes boredom is the real problem, and you can increase the interest by adding a new element—and soon have them cooperating again.

A lot of "naughtiness" is children just not knowing the right way to do things. Be prepared to teach rather than go on the attack when kids do something that isn't right.

For instance, picture a picnic table at the beach. A couple of families are eating together. The eight-year-old boy grabs the last three pieces of chicken from the dish with both hands. Parent number one yells, "Git out of there you hog!" and takes a swipe at him with a ladle. Good-humored, but not likely to change his behavior. Parent number two says, "Hold on, you haven't checked if anyone else wants some. How about you take one piece and eat that. Then ask later if the rest is free."

You teach your kids what good behavior is. How else will they find out?

Confronting

When you have tried all of the above and still your child is being difficult, then it may well mean that your child is asking for a confrontation. So why not give them one? Sometimes children set up conflicts from an inner need to experience safe, strong boundaries. At other times they just aren't able, without the help of our discipline, to handle a problem like sharing, waiting, not hitting, and so on. These are the times to use "stand and think." After all, a kid's life is pretty good, and it's not unfair if they have to cooperate sometimes whether they like it or not.

Whether the problem is sharing toys, being gentle, using words and not hitting, being patient, helping out, being obedient in an emergency, learning to join in a game, or whatever, "stand and think" followed by "dealing" helps them to stop their first impulse, think it through, and choose a course of action that is going to work. We are not aiming to "shut down" their behavior, but to make it more effective.

"So you wanted to join in the game the other kids were playing?" "Yep." "So you threw stones at the other children?" "Yep." "Did you notice that that didn't make them more friendly?" "Hmm!"

FROM TODDLER TO NICE PERSON IN THREE SHORT YEARS

RAISING LITTLE CHILDREN is easier if you have a goal to aim for. You are working on producing, by age five or so, a civilized little boy or girl who can go to school, stay at a friend's house, mix well with other kids, and talk to adults in a comfortable way. They'll still have lots to learn, but will be well on their way.

In our illustration above, the Stone Age Toddler, accustomed to being the "center of the known universe," starts in the left-hand position. That's all right for a little baby, but not good as a life plan. The aim of the discipline game is to have children over at the right-hand position by age five, ready to start school. Always remember that your child really wants to be kind, friendly, and cooperative–but needs help to learn how. Expect lots of repetition, but also a sense of steady progress. And always have lots of fun and good times in between the hassling.

All toddlers are difficult. You don't want to crush them just because they are showing strength. On the other hand, you don't want to always give in to them, because that teaches them that if they fuss and whine they will get their way. So it's a matter of being persistent and good-humored.

GETTING THE FIRMLOVE ATTITUDE

THE NEED FOR firmlove comes on in a big way when your child is around one and a half to two years old. The arrival of "naughtiness" can be disconcerting for the parent who just wants everything to be happy and gentle. Your baby shifts from an adorable if demanding little bundle to a mobile tank on legs.

It's a mental switch you just have to make. For parents of toddlers, firmlove involves realizing that while you have just spent the last eighteen months trying to make your child happy, you suddenly have quite the opposite situation. You must now, if you are doing your job, make them quite unhappy—dozens of times a day at first, though hopefully only for a few minutes at a time.

> *They will usually "help" you with this by choosing to do something really "unignorable," such as emptying the fridge or climbing into potted plants.*

The attitude you need is tough on the outside, relaxed on the inside. Don't let them think they are cute when they are being defiant or mischievous. It'll take weeks to undo the damage. Drop your voice, look serious, but at the same time feel good that they are learning a lot from having this discipline altercation.

> *While softlove opens a child's heart, firmlove gives them more backbone so that they will be strong and clear in the world as they grow up.*

WHAT IF I JUST GIVE IN
FOR THE SAKE OF PEACE AND QUIET?

ONE DAY AT the supermarket I decided that because my two-year-old daughter was fussing, I would let her get off the cart and walk around the aisles with me. This was a big mistake! She not only ran amok, she also expected the same thing for the next four shopping trips. Toddlers have memories like elephants!

Sometimes we want to take the easy way out. But this just teaches children to want more, and to complain and whine harder. Think about it from the two-year-old's point of view. They have been, for the first year, the absolute center of the universe. What they needed, they got. But now their wants have become more diverse and extreme. They don't just want to be fed, cuddled, and changed. They want to dress the dog in your pantyhose. They want to mix all the shampoo and conditioner into a slippery slide on the bathroom floor. They want to play in traffic. You have to stop them, if only for their own good.

And it is for their own good. Because one of the most important lessons of life is being learned at this age—that while you are loved and wanted, you are only one person among many and you have to get along with others, too.

Creating Likeable Kids, One Goal at a Time

JODIE, A participant in one of our courses, was very frank. "I don't like children," she said. "I've got three, and what I've found is that I just don't like kids after all!" This is a problem because if Jodie doesn't like her own children, how will anyone else like them? It's her job to turn them into kids that are likeable.

To help her, we get more specific. What changes will each child need to make so that Jodie can like them? We make a list.

1. Her two-year-old will stop hitting and biting.
2. Her four-year-old will stop whining and complaining.
3. Her five-year-old will learn to carry out instructions the first time he is asked.

Softlove comes before firmlove, and we realize that Jodie is quite exhausted. She will need time out for herself one day a week, as well as extra help from her husband. They resolve to give each other more care and attention, and practice firmlove skills together so they can back each other up. He will reduce his working hours from fifty hours a week to forty-five, in order to do this. Having well-behaved kids will make him happier to spend more time at home.

When we see Jodie six months later, she is looking much more relaxed and peaceful. Her life is still hard work, but she is being gentler on herself, and feeling much more successful with the kids.

✦

How Soon Does Discipline Begin?

GETTING DISCIPLINE TO work smoothly is easy if you understand what to expect and what is going to work at different ages.

Babies

Little Lukah doesn't need discipline. He is four months old. He is not yet able to crawl. He grins and plays with a rattle, and pulls things to himself. He also cries (many times a day) because he is a normal baby and that is how normal babies communicate their needs. His needs are simple—he cries when he is hungry, he cries when he is lonely, he cries when he is wet, he cries if his tummy hurts, and he cries when he is bored. That adds up to a lot of crying, but if his mom and dad are on the ball, they soon know what is probably needed and are in there at the first whimper to make things all right.

Lukah's dad explains that he was a very needy baby: "The big problem was getting him back to sleep—I had to put him on my shoulder and go for a walk around the neighborhood. Once at about 4 A.M. the police stopped me because I looked like a burglar with a bag of loot."

Babies can be hard work, but they are not being naughty—they are just trying to let you know their needs. They don't need discipline, just lots of understanding. And what parents need is sleep.

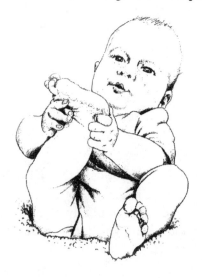

Toddlers

Babies' abilities quickly grow until soon they are crawling and then walking about, grabbing and pulling, chomping and poking everything in sight. The whole bottom third of your house is their domain. They are also discovering the use of words to make things happen—"Bottle!" "Gimme teddy!" "Hugga me!"

With new skills and mobility, your child is starting to do things and want things you can't possibly allow. So "misbehavior" emerges for the first time. A little baby doesn't deliberately misbehave—but a toddler is a different matter. Your toddler will walk over to the forbidden place or thing, and flash you a grin that says, "Whatya gonna do about it?" You say, "No," and they smile, "Oh yeah? Stop me."

Toddlers choose exactly what will "get your goat," because deep down they want to be stopped. This is an unconscious message saying, "I need some limits, Mom and Dad. Please stop me going berserk." (Teenagers too send this message, and we'll talk about them in a little while.)

It isn't all pure rebellion (though some of it is). Sometimes a toddler will just find it too hard to handle the demands of day-to-day life. Sometimes they will just be tired or hungry, and best put down for a sleep or given a snack—their mood will soon improve. Perhaps they will not want to be strapped into their car seat to go shopping when something good is going on in the yard. Or they will want to crawl across the dinner table to sample what's on their big brother's plate.

A kind parent uses all kinds of tricks to cajole a kid along, and a lot of the time this is just what is needed. For instance, one mother saved me a lot of trouble by explaining that if you give your toddler something delicious but time-consuming to eat when you go into the supermarket, they will sit happily in the shopping cart for twenty minutes. All the same, there will still be times when a child just has to be confronted and to do what you tell them to, because "I say so." This age is definitely the firmlove fiesta.

Preschoolers and Older Children

As children get beyond the toddler stage, you'll need to use "stand and think" far less often (thank goodness). Children will "deal" with you right away most of the time. Listen to their side of the story—what they were feeling or needing—as it might well be valid. If they can make a good case, then obviously you don't make them do things just because you want to be "the winner." They will learn that it's OK to have feelings or needs, but that sometimes they can't get what they want, or maybe they can if they go about it in a more acceptable way. Always find out from them what they were feeling (the feelings that led them to misbehave), and use firmlove in a kind way so that they know you really want to help, and not just persecute them.

Teenagers

Despite what people think, adolescents are generally beautiful, cooperative, interesting people. But they still need lots of involvement, and this includes some confrontations from time to time. It isn't right to use physical force with teenagers in any way, unless things are severe and you have professional help. So "stand and think" becomes "sit and talk." For example . . .

What time did you come in last night?
Uh, about one?

That's what I noticed. When did you agree you would be in by?
I said twelve, but it was hard to get a ride. The others wanted to stay.

So you couldn't get a ride and that made you late?
Yeah. Can I watch TV now?

Not so fast. How come you made a promise to me that you couldn't keep?
Well, I can't make the others bring me home!

Did you know that could happen when you made the promise?

Uhh, well, I didn't know.

So you made a deal you couldn't really keep.
Uhh, well, I guess so.

So how can we fix that in the future? You do want to go out in the future?
Huh! Yes I do!

. . . and so on.

In the brains of teenagers around thirteen years of age, everything is suddenly rewired. Puberty is setting in, and it makes them like newborn babies. They can become forgetful, disorganized, and slightly "batty." On the plus side, the changes combine to make them very "soft." Thirteen-year-olds can be trusting and affectionate—so it can be a chance to get close to them and rebond. Especially if you were hassled and busy when they were babies, this can be a time to build greater closeness.

Enjoy this time, because the "dopey thirteens" soon give way to the "cyclone season" of the fourteens. Fourteen-year-olds can be like emotional two-year-olds—testing limits, wanting to struggle with you, and needing you to struggle back. The last thing you should do is ignore them. They want independence but need to learn to be responsible and careful—a peak time for parenting input.

So for fourteen-year-olds, firmlove comes into play once again, only this time about different issues—what time to be home at night, picking up clothes, cooking meals for the family, and keeping promises and agreements. The methods of firmlove you use with teenagers are different from the ones you used with toddlers, but the principle is the same. "I will be firm with you, so you will learn to be a responsible person and know how to handle the real world," is what you are thinking. "No dishes, no dinner!" is what you are saying.

Teenagers are a big topic, which we can only touch on in this book. It is clear, though, that by getting softlove and firmlove working well with little children and school-age children, you will have a good foundation for handling adolescence when it comes along.

QUESTIONS PARENTS OFTEN ASK ABOUT "STAND AND THINK" AND "DEALING"

Q. What about a child who has not been disciplined much before, and is very naughty? I've tried lots of things and nothing works.
A. If you are introducing "stand and think" to a child who is very disobedient, then wait till you are ready. Make sure it is a good day when you have someone there to help you and are clear in your mind about what you want to achieve.

When and if a problem arises, give the child the chance to fix it. If they don't do that, explain that this will be a new way of dealing with problems. Walk them to the spot you have chosen and say something like, "You (threw the cake, hit your sister) and you have to stand here and think about it—why you did it, why it's a problem, and how you can fix it." If they try to move away, then hold them firmly, but safely, without hurting.

Expect some dramatics. It's a bit of a shock to an older child used to running amok. So decide to stay with it even through their loudness and struggling.

Always be firm without hurting. Say to them, "I will let you go when you stand still," then do it immediately when they comply.

Keep it simple and make it winnable. The first time, be happy with a small improvement—a quick "sorry" or a token effort is enough the first time.

They will calm down.

They will cooperate.

They will be praised for the new behavior.

And you can lie down afterward if you need to!

Next time, it will be a lot easier. Soon they will grow out of being difficult, and won't need more than a reminder to think about what they are doing and fix it.

Q. Should I hold them in the thinking spot if they won't stay there?
A. If they are little (one and a half to two and a half), allow them to sit or lie down—as long as they stay put. Stay close by and catch them and put them back if they try to "escape." You will probably need to do this only once or twice. When they are ready to talk, ask them to stand up and turn around to talk to you. An older child should stand quietly facing the wall, not propped up against it. Physically this keeps the child's attention on the one thing they should be thinking about. They literally aren't squirming around the problem, but are "standing up" to the task you have given them. Explain that only when he or she does this will you be willing to talk to them.

Q. How old should a child be when you use this method?
A. For you to be using this method, a child needs to have a certain amount of understanding and language. If they can say "Sorry," "Not hit," or "Hands off video" then they've got the message. Tell them they can come out now and get on with doing something pleasant. You can cuddle and calm them afterward, but don't make a big fuss. The aim is to let it go and get on with life. Until a child has these talking skills, you have to use baby methods, like diversion!

Q. Why stand up, and why use a corner?
A. This is for simple reasons. It cuts out other distractions and helps the child to focus. It is boring to face the wall, and legs get tired in a minute or so just standing still. It isn't meant to be either painful or embarrassing. The aim is to get the child motivated to solve the problem and get out of there. Tell him or her, "You don't have to feel bad, you're there to think about what you should have done. As soon as you

have figured it out, we'll talk and you can come out."

Away from home, or once your child is really used to standing still when told to, you don't need a wall or corner. You can simply say, "Stand there and think," in any location.

Q. My child says he's sorry, and then does it all over again.

A. The older they get, the more they test you—it's the sign of a smart kid. Expect the following confidence tricks:

+ I can't stand and think—I have to go to the bathroom.
+ You don't understand me.
+ You don't love me.
+ I can't remember.

Don't be fooled. They have to convince you (before you let them out) that they really are feeling sorry and really are going to change. Through watching their body language, and through being alert during the dealing conversation, you will soon know if they are being genuine.

Q. Can schools use this method?

A. Yes, but only with some important modifications. "Stand and think" would be humiliating in front of peers other than brothers and sisters in a family setting. Many elementary schools we have consulted around the world now use a "thinking place," which is a chair, mat, stool, or beanbag. The thinking place isn't especially conspicuous, and shouldn't have a humiliating name like "naughty chair," nor should it be used as punishment or to single a child out. The thinking place is used to remove a child from the action, give them time and motivation to think, and keep them close by where you can see from their body language if they are ready to "deal."

And always a teacher or principal should deal with them soon. It isn't a sentence they are serving. Kids who misbehave do need your attention, so give it to them through dealing with what happened. Remember to also give them attention when they are doing the right thing.

Often in a school setting, the best thing is to let things cool for just a minute or two, then have a roundtable discussion with the children involved. The teacher helps the children to "deal," or to mediate a way out of conflict—to try and meet the feelings and needs of all involved.

WHAT ABOUT THE OLD WAYS OF DISCIPLINE?

THERE HAS BEEN a gradual evolution of discipline techniques in the last fifty years.

Hitting and Hurting

This was the old way. It made children frightened, it eroded any loving relationship, and it taught children that it's OK to hit if you are bigger. Children who were hit became fearful or broken-spirited, or they got angrier and struck back. Sometimes when these children grew up, their own children, wives, and others became victims of the anger that had been stored in their bodies. Violent methods are harmful and have no benefit. In some countries, they are against the law.

Shaming and Blaming

When parents rightly began to reject hitting and smacking in the 1950s, they sometimes had no other tools to put in their place, and few skills in communication. So they often used shame, fear, blame—calling their children no good and a million other names. The result was a damaged self, a wounding of the spirit. Shaming and blaming were often a failure as discipline too, because children became what they were called–lazy, stupid, selfish, fat, whatever. Kids who were shamed went one of two ways–either depressed and guilty, or rebellious and angry.

Rewards and Consequences

A good example of these are star charts, where a child gets stars for good behavior, usually building up to some reward at the end of the week or when they have enough stars. Star charts can work well because they help parents focus on the positive and they help the child have smaller goals to aim for. With some children this can make a lot of difference.

Pocket money in a small quantity, some jobs that you just "have to" do as your part in the family, and extra pay for doing extra jobs, is a mix of rewards that many families have found works well because it resembles the real world.

Similarly, "natural consequences" work by letting the child suffer the consequences of the problem they create–changing the sheets if they wet the bed, getting into trouble if they are late for school, and so on. As children get older, they are more and more able to learn from the results of their actions and it is important for parents to allow this to happen. Natural consequences aren't enough on their own–for example, letting the child experience the consequence of running across the street without looking both ways would not be a good idea.

Time-Out

Time-outs have become a popular recommendation of parenting experts. It means sending your child to their room, usually for about five minutes, to cool off. It has literally saved a lot of children's lives, because it gives parents time to cool off too. So it is a coping strategy, and useful to almost everyone at times. I use it myself with a toddler when I am hot and bothered and just want some peace for a few minutes. But, by itself, a time-out is not a discipline method because it doesn't involve teaching or thinking about change.

Here are some examples of what parents tell us about time-outs: "It doesn't work because my children have fun in their room, they have so many toys!," or "He smashes the room up, breaks things, and sometimes climbs out of the window," or "It works well for me—mainly as a chance to cool off. But it doesn't always change the behavior. She often just does it all again ten minutes later."

The key differences between a "time-out" and "stand and think" are:

1. *"Stand and think" is quicker. When the child is in the corner in the same room with you, you are able to see right away when they have finished thinking about their behavior. It encourages rapid resolution.*
2. *There are no distractions with "stand and think." The child stays put until they do the thinking they need to do. It keeps the problem with the child.*
3. *"Stand and think" isn't a punishment. It's a thinking and teaching time. It doesn't create resentment. The child can end the process by cooperating at any time, and so is usually out within a minute or two.*
4. *"Dealing" creates closeness, not distance. Naughty kids don't need isolation—they usually need more intense contact. The dealing conversation shows that you care, and you want to help them solve their problems.*

We recommend that you use a time-out only if you feel you are in danger of hitting your child, or otherwise really need a break. In fact, you can use it preventively by saying, "I want us both to cool down now. Please go to your room and play quietly." You may wish to have a "dealing" conversation afterward, so that you know something has changed.

HELPING OLDER CHILDREN WITH MORAL DECISIONS

SOME CHILDHOOD DILEMMAS aren't so much discipline questions as values questions. You want your children to decide for themselves what is the right thing to do. You can't make kids take on your values. But you can help them figure out all the angles of their behavior. In the long run, this means they will do the right thing when you are not around, because they believe it is the right thing.

Sara, aged nine, was asked by a friend to go to her slumber party. She happily agreed. Her friend, a shy girl, was really pleased that Sara had accepted–there were only three girls attending.

Then, out of the blue, Sara was invited to a church camping weekend by another friend–but it clashed with the date of the party. Sara really wanted to go camping, but it meant breaking her word that she would go to the slumber party. Her parents didn't force her to keep the agreement–that would have just led to sulking. But they discussed the two parts of the problem with her:

1. Respecting her friend's feelings.
2. Keeping an agreement.

These were important principles. Sara's parents gently pointed out that "something better has come up" is no excuse for disappointing someone who is counting on you. They also said it was Sara's decision, and they wouldn't hassle her once she had decided. Sara reluctantly declined the camping trip, and had fun at the slumber party. Her parents felt really proud of her for showing so much character.

Children and teenagers won't always make the decision you are hoping for. But making mistakes is part of the lesson. Also, it's just remotely possible that you might be wrong and that they might be right–a sobering thought!

SHOULD I SMACK?–AN IMPORTANT DECISION EVERY PARENT HAS TO MAKE

IT'S GETTING DARK, and the highway is heavy with traffic going home for the night. People hurry along the sidewalk and a light rain has begun to fall. A little child's yelling catches my attention—a young mother is talking at a pay phone outside a shop, and at the same time trying to keep her toddler in check. He wants to run and play at the curb, where rainwater is gurgling and splashing. But the cars and trucks are dangerously close by. You can feel her frustration—she is alternately raging angrily with whomever is on the phone, then shouting at her youngster that she will "teach him to behave." He complains and struggles to pull free. Then it's all too much. She drops the phone, grabs the neck of his tiny windbreaker, and gives him a backhanded blow across the face that makes his head spin.

Attitudes Have Changed

It used to be an everyday event, forty or fifty years ago, to see children being beaten by adults. People did it in public, and nobody so much as batted an eyelash. Attitudes toward hitting children have changed, just as they have changed to men hitting women. Today, a bruised child is a police matter. Eighty percent of parents say they still smack their children occasionally, but most would prefer not to.

There are still many people though (usually men) who advocate a smack as a way to get quick results. Perhaps it's time for us to make a personal choice about what happens to our kids— especially now that better forms of discipline are available to us. We believe that if parents knew of a better form of discipline, they would never smack again.

Are beating and smacking the same? Isn't smacking just a little bit of needed discipline? Often when I give a talk about discipline, someone will come up to me and say, "I got plenty of hidings when I was a kid, and they never hurt me!" My guess— based partly on the very passion with which these people speak— is that it did hurt them, and it still is hurting. Pretending it didn't hurt is the child's first defense against humiliation. And the anger they hold inside comes out later in many different ways.

It's time we were more honest about this whole issue. From a child's viewpoint, smacking is scary and humiliating. From a parent's point of view, it is risky. Risky because there isn't any clear-cut point where a smack becomes a hit, and a hit becomes an angry venting of parental frustration. How do we know how much is enough? Can we honestly say when we are hitting for the child's "benefit," and when it's just to make us feel better? Or to get revenge? Can we honestly say it's just the child we're angry with, and not a lot of things rolled into one?

The bottom line is that smacking really doesn't work, except in the very short term. It eats away at love and trust–so children get crankier still. I have seen many children–who defiantly say, "It didn't hurt! I don't care!"–learn to become immune to it. The parents who smack their children on the street or in the supermarket are clearly losing control of their children, not gaining it.

Why Do Parents Smack Their Kids?

The fact of it is–if we're honest–we hit children because of our own needs. We are scared of losing control over them. Or often with young children, our nurturing energy just runs out. We feel exhausted, sleep-deprived, we never have a moment to ourselves. The slap is just our inner self striking back, saying "I've got needs too." It can be a self-protection instinct–they've just jabbed you in the eye as you put them in their car seat, or banged you with a spoon as you straightened their bib.

At this age, children can't always understand or notice our feelings or our words to them. Yet we feel a strong urge to make an impact, to have an effect on their behavior. So smacking or hitting them to "get their attention" is a natural urge. We need to resist this urge, and can do so if we improve our skills in connecting with our children and making them take notice.

Some smacking advocates are compassionate and concerned people. They sometimes argue that if not controlled early by a light tap, children will become even naughtier, until a mom or dad loses all patience and really hits them hard. The theory is that little hits prevent the need for big ones. However, parents have often told me that little hits and smacks soon don't work, as they insult and affront the dignity of the child so much that they begin to say "that didn't hurt"—and you are faced with hitting them harder. When parents are really stressed, they often hit harder or more often than they really would have wished to. It can be a terrifying feeling of losing control. Also, kids get resentful, they hit their own brothers and sisters, or hit you back. It's important to draw the line, and the realistic place to draw it is back at square one. If we decide never to hit our children—as I and many people I know have done—then we are committed to finding better ways.

Discipline Without Smacking

We do have to discipline children. And words alone are not enough with very little ones. It's certainly necessary to sometimes hold and restrain little children to help them to calm down and behave. This can be done quite safely. "Stand and think" has been adopted successfully by thousands of parents. It's a matter of training your child as he or she grows up. And there will still be "impossible" times in the rain on the street, where it's just a matter of "pick up and carry." You have to keep your sense of humor. It's lucky toddlers are small—it makes them portable.

By the time adolescence comes along, there should never be any need for fear or intimidation. If kids run away from home, or are violently defiant, this almost always means that communication has broken down years back, and parents have been relying on aggression rather than a mixture of love and assertiveness.

Many people block out the memory of the pain they felt as children—and so go on inflicting this pain on their kids. As a counselor, I know what pain is involved. I have heard too many people talk—with tears in their eyes—about the humiliation and fear they felt when a parent went out of control. My patients show me the broken blood vessels in their legs from being "smacked" as children. Hairdressers tell me many of their clients have nicks and bare spots and scars under their hairline from blows on the head when they were little. The scars are even bigger on the inside—if children cannot feel safe and secure with their own parents, how can they feel safe in the world?

There's another reason to stop hitting children. Evidence is mounting that children who feel safe with their parents will tell their parents if something is wrong—for instance, if they have been sexually assaulted. When parents routinely use fear and shame as discipline tools, then children will feel unsafe to tell, in case they are blamed. Kids who are never frightened or harmed by their parents will always see their parents primarily as protectors. They will feel safer to say, "No—I'll tell!" to somebody else, and avoid abuse in the first place.

Making the Decision

We think that it is time for us as parents to abandon hitting as a way of controlling children.

The first step is simple. You make a personal commitment never to hit a child again. The automatic effect is that you become committed to finding nonviolent discipline methods that work. Such methods exist, and can be mastered.

While raising our first child, we found ourselves giving little smacks for certain behavior—things like touching the heater. Being a strong-willed child, our son was not impressed by this and made a habit of repeating the behavior. We found that we were miserable about making him cry, and we weren't teaching him much either. So we began to search for alternatives. We discovered that some parents never smacked their children, and that in fact there were whole countries, like Sweden, Finland, Denmark, and Norway, where it was illegal to smack a child. We also learned the firm and clear forms of discipline taught in this book, and used by thousands of parents around the world, and began putting them into practice in our home. We are eternally grateful to have found a better way.

We are all yearning for a peaceful world—where conflicts can be negotiated nonviolently. We need to start at the beginning. If we can't manage it at home, we will never manage it in the Middle East.

If you find yourself in agreement, you can make this commitment too. Your children will come to know that their mother or father will never, ever, physically harm them. That they are safe in their own home. What a beautiful way to be.

CONCLUSION

BY USING FIRMLOVE methods, you can win both ways. You can give up on smacking and blaming, which no one really enjoys. And yet you can have a household where the adults are in charge, and the kids do what they are told when necessary. Your kids will still be normal—two-year-olds will still be hard work, and fourteen-year-olds will still be cyclonic. But by knowing |how to respond you can address these stages confidently and clearly, and then get on with the enjoyable and pleasant parts of family life.

Remember—always and only do what works best for you. "Stand and think" and "dealing" are just two more possible strings to your bow. As this letter from a family indicates, they can make a lot of difference:

Dear Steve and Shaaron,

We attended your seminar in October, and thoroughly enjoyed the session. I still keep in touch with another lady I met there.

Your seminar came at an appropriate time because we didn't want to beat our son Carey, but didn't know what to do. Now Carey (twenty-eight months) stands himself in "the corner" and says "I'm thinking about it" and the tears in our eyes are from joy—he's so cute!

Marion and David

❖ **four** ❖

Who Will Raise Your Children?

TAKING CARE WITH CHILD CARE

✦

It's 9:30 IN the morning when the phone rings. On the line is a young professional woman whom I know only slightly. She is in tears. She has just left her four-month-old baby boy at a child-care center for the first time, and is now sitting at her desk on her first day back at work.

The baby was distressed to be left, she was anguished to leave him. She can't concentrate on her work—all she can think of is her baby, who has scarcely been away from her in his whole short life. What should she do?

DOING WHAT YOUR HEART SAYS

MANY PEOPLE WOULD say to the young mother returning to work, "What's the problem? The child will soon settle down." After all, this can happen with a five-year-old, too, on their first day at school, and they are usually soon over it and settling in happily. Shouldn't she just put it out of her mind and concentrate on her job and her coworkers?

As we talk it over, it emerges that it isn't just a problem of a tearful parting. This young woman has a deep ambivalence about returning to work.

We discuss the pressures on her, trying to separate what are her own feelings and what are the wishes of others around her. Many of her friends have their babies cared for in day-care centers and are working. Her husband wants her to go back to work—the money will be welcome. Her employer wants her back at work—she has been away only five months total.

But as she talks, it's clear that she is not happy. What she wants is to be with her child. Gradually, she begins to settle on what she will do. She decides to meet with her boss and explain that she has changed her plans, to apologize for this, and thank him for being understanding. After negotiation with her boss, she in fact takes a whole further year off, and then returns only part-time. She's lucky—to be a skilled person, and to have a partner whose income can support the family—so that she can choose to do this. She is enormously relieved to be following her own heart, and not the "shoulds" put onto her by society and those around her.

Child Care—A New Invention

From time immemorial, most children have been raised close to home by a combination of their parents and close relatives, in a village or neighborhood setting. So the work (and the pleasure) of raising children was shared among those who loved them. Throughout the nonindustrial world even today, children and adults spend their days together. You will see mothers at work with babies in slings, and little children accompanying men to work in the fields. It is only in the Western world that we shut our children (and our elderly) away from the mainstream of life.

For centuries, men worked with their families close by almost all the time. Even a hundred years ago, 97 percent of American men worked within walking distance of their home.

Then, with industrialization, men began to travel to distant work, leaving women and children, often isolated and lonely, at home. In the sixties women decided they wanted to work too, and joined men in a flight from the home.

Reduced wages, single parenthood, and unemployment have meant that many women have to work in addition to raising a family. To deal with this, there has been a rapid upsurge in child-care provisions of various kinds. Today, we talk of the child-care "industry," and finding suitable child-care is a subject close to the heart of almost every parent.

So today's parents have an option that in the past was only available to the extremely wealthy. We can pay professionals to take care of our children all day. If you can overcome the problems of waiting lists, the cross-city drives, and your fears about quality of care, then encouraged by strong ideologies about your rights to do so, you may have your children cared for from birth to adulthood by complete strangers. (Once at school they can have before- and after-school care, vacation care, and weekend learning camps. You hardly need to see them!)

We know that approximately two and a half million young children are in full-time day care in the U.S., and many children will spend up to 12,000 hours there before they reach school age.

THE SECOND BIGGEST DECISION A PARENT MAKES

THE DECISION TO have children is probably the biggest decision you ever make in your life. Deciding who will raise your children is the second biggest. We use the word "raise" because the first five years are well known to be the time of maximum intellectual and emotional growth. Children who go into care at two or three months of age, and stay for seven or eight hours a day, are basically spending their childhood in care. What kind of person they become—how they are comforted, how they are disciplined, what values and attitudes they will take on—will be the composite of the input of a large number of people, with widely varying styles and values. These children will certainly be adaptable! But will they be capable of intimacy? How will they integrate all these messages?

The two big questions—whether to have children, and who will care for them—are linked. As more than one day-care director has told us in private (after fighting off the pressure from parents to take younger and younger babies for longer and longer hours), "I don't know why some of these people have children at all!" It's a fair comment.

THE CUCKOO CULTURE

IN THE LAST ten years a kind of "cuckoo culture" has developed. (Cuckoos are birds that lay their eggs in other birds' nests to be raised by them.) This trend has been encouraged through young women's magazines, and by media role models who portray this lifestyle as ideal. In some circles, having your kids raised for you is seen as a measure of success—the desirable norm.

We are a society that worships "freedom," including freedom from the inconvenience of children. At the extreme end of the spectrum, there are sections of American society where children have become little more than a fashion accessory—window dressing—wheeled out for a photo opportunity and then shuffled off to be attended to by others. It's fashionable to "have" kids, but not necessarily to be encumbered by them.

We humans are very conformist creatures, and the perception that "everyone does it" makes child care as a choice seem harmless or even beneficial. So fashion, as much as real hard data, often influences these important decisions.

While the growth of this "arm's-length" parenting is a worry, the vast majority of parents are not like this. Most parents do want to raise their own children, do want the best for them, and are willing to sacrifice career aspirations and recreational or social goals to a high degree to achieve these aims. Increasingly, men—even those in public life—are making decisions that favor parenthood over career.

Sadly, many parents feel forced by economic need to return to work when their children are young. They do so with immense regret. Others are confused, wanting to provide a nice home, toys, school fees, but not wanting to miss out on time with their children either. Whatever the reason, we need to know the real cost before making a decision.

A Personal View . . .
and What the Newest Research Shows

I HAVE ALWAYS felt uneasy seeing babies and toddlers in day care—the unnaturalness of the large numbers of children, the noisy and more impersonal atmosphere, the struggles of staff to meet children's needs. I also have strong concerns that day care is being used for younger and younger babies, and for longer periods of time. This is a change in the way we rear children on a huge scale, and the results may not be known until they are too late to reverse.

I am not alone in this view. Since as far back as 1986, Professor Jay Belsky, arguably the leading researcher in the field, tentatively reversed his long-standing support of day care for children under three. Then, in 1994, one of the world's most respected child-development authors, Dr. Penelope Leach, created a storm of concern by criticizing the use of day care for babies and toddlers in her book *Children First*. In an attempt to resolve the controversy, a landmark study was initiated by the U.S. National Institute of Child Health and Development (NICHD), involving the nation's leading researchers with viewpoints all along the spectrum. It was a better designed and more thorough study than had ever been conducted before. Its findings, released in 2002, confirmed our fears, and shocked many who had been complacent in the child-development field. It emerged that small but measurable damage was being done to a significant number of children by the early use of day care. By the time they entered grade school, day-care kids were found to be somewhat more aggressive, more antisocial, more insecure, and poorer learners. As well as affecting their social adjustment and learning abilities, some children with more vulnerable bonds to their mothers had these bonds weakened or damaged. The differences were not huge, but they were definitely there, and most importantly of all, they were *independent of the quality of the care,* which had previously been thought to be a safeguarding factor.

What are parents to do with these findings? There is one clear implication—to use day care less. The greatest effect on children's well-being occurred when there were three factors in combination—child care that started too early, was used for too many hours each day, and went on for too many years continuously. Too much, too early, too long. And how much was too much? There was no reassuring distinct cutoff point—to quote the researchers, the damage was "dose-dependent." In other words, the more day care was used, the greater the risk of negative effects. Day care didn't destroy children, it was more a matter of eroding their development little by little. It was like a diet that just wasn't nourishing enough. Overdependence on child care made for a second-class childhood.

Many more questions remain. For instance, we know nothing about the big, long-term questions—whether there are effects on these children's ability to form good marriages, on their own abilities as parents, their long-term mental health, and so on. And sadly, none of us can press a pause button on our children's lives until the studies are all finished. We have to take in the information, together with what our own hearts and minds are telling us, based on our situation and our own particular child. One child might be robust enough to handle what another would be devastated by.

My belief, now backed by considerable research evidence, is that except in those cases of parents who are seriously impaired or genuinely incapable of raising their own children, *young children under three are almost always better off being cared for by someone who loves them.* Professionalism of staff and richness of surroundings, while important, don't touch on the question of love. Young children's bodies can be kept safe and their minds occupied, but their deeper and more subtle needs cannot be met other than by someone with a fierce, long-term commitment to them as individuals. This is not something money can buy.

THE PLUSES OF CHILD CARE

THE DANGERS OF child care suggested above have to be set alongside its benefits. It's clear to anyone associated with families:

+ That all parents need breaks from the lonely and unnatural world of being at home alone with little children.
+ That women have as much right as men to have and develop careers, and to be economically independent.
+ That children in day care learn social and other skills, have enriched input and stimulation, and in many cases love and enjoy their time in day-care centers, family day care, or other child-care situations.
+ That some parents are so ill equipped (materially or personally) that children are safer, happier, and better off being cared for professionally for most of the time.

These pluses are well documented, and widely accepted.

FEARLESSLY FACING THE FACTS

THE PLUSES ARE real, but so are the minuses. For a long time, however, the minuses have been suppressed—for fear of making parents feel guilty, or for fear of inviting even closer scrutiny and questioning of the child-care "industry." I think the first reason is patronizing, and the second is dishonest.

Child-care professionals often have a well-intentioned, but (I think) misplaced tendency to protect parents from concern. For example, in Australia there has been a long and important campaign by child-care academics and government centers to bring in national standards of child care. This campaign was vigorously opposed by the private sector of the industry. A spokeswoman supporting better standards was quoted as saying, "We didn't want to create hysteria by emphasizing cases where untrained fifteen-year-olds were left in charge of forty-five children." The intention is admirable, but why should parents be seen as more hysterical than any other group? Parents care intensely about their children, and should be informed.

Is the rapid and widespread adoption of child care a terrible thing? Or is it a wonderful breakthrough for parents—setting them free to have a better life? Is it a boon for children, given that many of us no longer live close to grandparents and relatives, who used to take this role, to have professionals to care for them (instead of amateurs like their mom and dad)? Or does it represent a serious loss of intimacy and specialness in childhood? Taking a middle road: can child care be used in a balanced way to augment and enhance early childhood? However we view it, the child-care boom is a huge, uncontrolled social experiment, and needs to be looked at with very clear eyes.

In this chapter we'll look at the reasons why people go back to work when their children are little, and whether these reasons are realistic. We'll discuss whether it actually makes more sense—and brings more joy—to stay home for a few years until your children are older.

Then we'll look at the realities of what care is available so that when you do need it, you can choose wisely. We'll examine what the hazards of child care are so that you can analyze whether your child is suffering ill effects. We believe that once you are armed with this information, you will be better able to make a choice that is right for you.

⌣ "But What If I Have No ∿ Choice?"—Mothers Who Are Forced to Work

*M*ANY MOTHERS with low-income-earning (or unemployed) partners, or single mothers, simply have no choice but to work, even though they would strongly prefer to be with their children.

My belief is that children can adapt to difficult circumstances if they understand the necessity. They can also intuit the truth. If your children know you would rather be with them, but that you have no choice, then the effect on their self-esteem is not nearly as severe as if they feel you just aren't interested in them—that you would rather be somewhere else.

✦

UNDERMINING THE CONFIDENCE OF YOUNG PARENTS

SOMETIMES YOUNG PARENTS returning to work will argue that they are not "good" at parenting–that their child would be better off with a caregiver. Yet it isn't as simple as being a good or bad parent–very few of us are good at it to begin with. Through the hours spent together, you become a good parent for that child. That's what a relationship (as opposed to a service) is all about.

Child care can actually undermine your confidence. Sometimes parents feel that it makes the situation worse. They lose confidence and can be made to feel alienated from their child, not as loving, as capable, or as interesting as the caregiver. The better others seem able to handle your baby or toddler, the lower your self-esteem sinks. It is more helpful to work with a parent–to give them skills, teach them more positive interactions, and to care for them–than to bypass them and care for the baby. It's a sensitive question.

Stability and consistency, the underpinnings of a young child's world, seem impossible to attain in child care. Even "quality" care still means your child gets looked after by dozens of different individuals in the course of the four or so years before starting school. In reality, we cannot even have our children looked after in one location–a recent study found that some families had to access up to four different kinds of care in an average week to cover the hours they needed. Another study found great inconsistencies between centers, that children had to deal with during a normal day.

FINDING A BALANCE THAT ISN'T A COMPROMISE

LIFE WITH TODDLERS in a lonely suburban house or apartment can be a recipe for insanity if it is unrelieved by adult contact and activities other than housekeeping and parenting. So for the well-being of adults and children, we need ways of providing safe care.

Friends, family day care, and child-care centers can all work well, at different times of a child's life in different combinations, to improve a family's life greatly. The key is to know what children's real needs are. This has been the missing piece in the discussion so far. Child care was invented for the convenience of adults, not the needs or wishes of children. Those were an afterthought.

Research evidence, along with a revival of plain common sense, is leading to a reversal of the idea that a day-care childhood is a good childhood. I predict that there will be a definite move toward the use of child care to augment parenting (rather than, as it is sometimes used today, as a virtual replacement for it). I also predict (and hope) that the use of child care for babies and toddlers will be drastically reduced as parents realize the psychological and other costs.

As we leave the "you can have it all" thinking of the late twentieth century and enter the more thoughtful and sober realities of the twenty-first century, we are taking a fresh look at many things, and one of these is how we raise our children. The long lines for child-care placement may soon be a thing of the past, as people begin to stream in the other direction—heading for a more human and less materialistic life.

NEWS RELEASE

"Working mothers who send their young children to child-care centers may suffer from high levels of depression because of the separation, a new study has found. Some mothers lapsed into a depression serious enough to justify treatment by a psychiatrist, the study revealed.

"About eighty Melbourne mothers, who were putting their infants aged under two in suburban day care centers while working for financial needs, were interviewed by a University of Melbourne researcher. The study found that within the first two months of using childcare, many women complained of anxiety after being separated from their children. The anxiety sometimes led to depression. Four of the eighty women were suffering from severe clinical depression.

"About one in three of the working Moms said they would have preferred to have stayed at home with their child instead of working and leaving their child in day care.

"Another group of eighty mothers who stayed at home to care for their children did not show the same levels of anxiety."

("Working Moms feel the pain of leaving children," the Mercury, *13 February 1993)*

◡ Seven Shameless Reasons ᷍ for Staying Home When Your Kids Are Small

1. **I'm selfish**—why should someone else enjoy my beautiful children while I slave away to pay for it? Why should they enjoy seeing them take their first steps and say new words? Why should someone else get that glorious affection my children give out? I want it for me!

2. **I'm the best**—no one can raise my kids as well as I can. No one feels about them the way I do. No one knows them like I do.

3. **I'm super cautious**—I'm fastidious about safety, about guarding against abuse, about sensitivity to their feelings and what media they are exposed to. By being

around all the time, I don't have to take chances on these issues—I know they are safe.

4. **I enjoy working in a team**—my partner and I work together well, we complement each other in parenting, and I like doing this with him/her. It's something else that makes us closer.

5. **I'm poor and proud**—I have so much self-esteem that I don't need great furniture or expensive clothes or a fancy house and car. I'm such a snob that I don't need money beyond the bare essentials. My kids are my jewelry.

6. **I'm lazy**—by raising secure and hassle-free kids who feel safe and settled, I am making it easy for myself later on. I'm planning to cruise through their adolescence. And I'm teaching them fifty kinds of housework.

7. **I'm "into it"**—I enjoy the progress, the affection, the freedom to set my own pace, to decide how I will spend my time, the social get-togethers with other parents, the effect of the seasons on our activities, how my kids keep me young, and that I am (for this short time) the center of their world.

WHY PARENTS CHOOSE CHILD CARE

THERE ARE FOUR main reasons why parents return to work.

1. Real financial need

Many families need both parents to be employed to survive. Many single mothers, too, need to work to provide adequately for their kids. For these families, child care is a necessity of life. In one survey, 62 percent of employed mothers indicated they would prefer to stay at home while children are below school age.

2. Perceived financial need

Many couples feel that they need to work, but on closer examination this is based on a desire for a relatively high standard of living. As couples marry later and have children later, perhaps they have grown used to a high disposable income. A few decades ago, "going without" was a normal part of life with young children and less of a concern. Our media images and expectations, and a competitive rather than supportive kind of society, mean that standards of income are much higher than what is actually required.

3. Peer pressure

Many mothers feel they "should" go to work, that this is "the thing to do," and that they are somehow defective if they "just" want to raise children. Feminism has been ambiguous about motherhood, and the nurturing of children has sometimes been devalued. For a man to prefer parenting to the full-time paid workforce is also seen as rather unusual.

4. Enjoyment of career

Some mothers find their career so satisfying and enjoyable that it competes favorably with being at home with children.

Sometimes their partner is more interested in full-time parenting, and so they reverse roles. At other times neither partner is so keen on being with the children, and they place their children lower in their priorities.

Whereas it was once the case that mothers who could afford to remain at home during the earliest years of their children's lives did so until school enrollment or perhaps a year or two earlier, American mothers today who re-enter the labor force after having a baby now routinely do so in the child's first year—even months—of life. As a result, by 1990, rates of maternal employment for married mothers of three-years-olds and of six-month-olds were virtually indistinguishable in the U.S. Whereas roughly 38 percent of mothers of infants under one year of age were in the labor force in 1980, by 1990 the figure had risen to 55 percent where it basically remains today. (U.S. Bureau of Census, 1999)

IF YOU DO HAVE A CHOICE BUT JUST DON'T LIKE PARENTING

THE AVAILABILITY OF child care from babyhood has meant that many people decide to have children, while planning to have the bulk of their care done by others. Other parents feel that they are not really very good at parenting, and so it is better done by others.

But the fact is, many of us are not good parents to begin with. It comes with practice. Parenthood isn't a hobby, and it isn't a fair-weather kind of thing. There may be whole stages of the life cycle that you find very difficult—not all mothers like babies, some people find toddlers impossible, others dislike teenagers, and so on. Every parent at some time feels like giving up and retreating.

But there are usually reasons behind this that are worth getting to the bottom of.

It's in facing up to many crises and not giving in that we learn and come to really know ourselves and find how to be with children in a satisfying and happy way.

IS THERE A CHILD CARE SYNDROME? (HOW CAN I TELL IF CHILD CARE IS HARMING MY CHILD?)

IN THE SIXTIES, there was some concern about whether institutional child care harmed children. However, the research seemed reassuring—on the measures used, there was little if any difference. If anything, children in day care were more socially skilled, and somewhat more independent and assertive. Critics of these studies pointed out that almost all of them were of high-quality centers, usually on university campuses convenient to the researchers, and far from representative of the real world.

So in the seventies, the direction swung to investigating what was meant by "quality," and whether this made a difference. It was found, not surprisingly, that smaller groups, better educated caregivers, and high staff ratios all improved the outcomes. There was a risk identified of "apathy and distress" among infants in larger groups, and "boredom and tuning out" among older children if programs were not well designed.

In the eighties, researchers began to suspect that the kind of quality care parents want for their children just might not be possible in a formal setting. Why not? A secure, warm attachment to caregivers emerges again and again as the problem area. Kids get attached to a particular caregiver. Being able to form attachments that are lasting and based on trust are at the heart of learning to be human. Yet here in the U.S., there is a 40 percent annual turnover rate among day-care staff—largely due to the stress and poor conditions and pay. (What other industry would have this huge staff turnover? Fruit-picking?) For a child, the loss of a familiar person they are attached to is very painful. Yet in a childhood spent with every weekday in day care, this will happen over and over again.

In a penetrating and careful article, "Infant Day Care, a Cause for Concern," Jay Belsky (whom we mentioned earlier) analyzed the entire body of research, collected from hundreds of studies from around the world in all imaginable conditions.

He found that there were suggestions of specific and recurrent damaging effects that emerged in many studies, which, if not proven, were strongly indicated, especially when the research picture was looked at as a whole. In particular, he found four outcomes that were of concern in children who had entered child care before the age of one:

+ A pattern of withdrawal from and avoidance of the mother figure–babies and toddlers who did not approach their mothers, or see their mothers as sources of reassurance. The child-care experience seemed to make these little ones angry at their mothers, so that they did not turn to her for comfort. Their attachment was either displaced elsewhere, or they did not form strong attachments.
+ Heightened aggressiveness–a tendency in the present, as well as later in school life, to use aggression, hitting, swearing, and fighting, rather than talking through, walking away, staying calm.
+ Noncompliance–ignoring or defying adults' requests or commands, doing the opposite, being rebellious.
+ Social withdrawal–walking away, avoiding adult company, keeping to themselves.

These four effects were found across a wide range of studies—impoverished, middle class, upper class, in unstable family day care, high-quality centers, poor-quality centers, and even with at-home baby-sitter care.

The effects are not surprising. Placed in the average child-care center where other children compete for attention, where adult figures come and go, where the day is noisy and there is no private space, children learn to fend for themselves. They may learn not to place too much trust in adult figures, including their own mother, who is not there for them for much of the day. They cope as best they can, some probably better than others.

For parents, then, the question, "Is child care harming my child?" can be answered with some clarity. If the child is regularly displaying a combination of the four symptoms listed above, then the answer is probably "Yes."

"You Can Spot the Child-Care Kids"

WHILE RESEARCHING and interviewing parents for this section, we came across some revealing comments from parents who were also elementary and preschool teachers.

"You can tell which kids have been in day care before starting school. They are really different."

"It's hard to describe—they are kind of colder, less interested in you as a person. They can be quite good at manipulation."

"Most little ones come along holding Mommy's hand—they are anxious, but they soon pass on the trust from their mother to you (the teacher). They are very affectionate and contactable. Child-care children seem kind of hardened—it's just another person, just another place. You often don't meet their parents either. They might have come from day care, and go back to it after school."

"You get the impression these children have met lots of adults, and have no special feeling about it anymore. They function all right, get on with the day, but it's with a kind of resigned feeling. They are tougher, almost depressed."

COMPARING THE OPTIONS

THERE ARE MANY kinds of child-care options to choose from. Each has pluses and minuses. Let's look at each in turn so you can evaluate which, if any, are suited to your needs.

What Is a Child-Care Center Like?

Most centers are purpose-built buildings about the size of a large house. They usually open from 8:00 A.M. to 6:00 P.M. or longer if they cater to parents who work the late shift. They may offer full-time, part-time, and occasional care. Regulations govern staff numbers, children's numbers, space indoors and out, toilets, and so on.

Staff ratios are about one adult to five under-two-year-olds, and one to fifteen over-twos. Some of the staff, but not all, need to have child-care or early childhood qualifications. Good centers will provide structured programs similar to preschool activities so that children can learn through guided activity and play.

Fees vary from center to center in the U.S., but average well over $100 per week. In some circumstances a portion of this cost is covered by government subsidy, in others it falls completely on the parents.

Child care can be both expensive and cheap, depending on your point of view and your circumstances. The government estimates the average annual cost of full-time child care is $5,280 per child, which is almost a quarter of the after-tax income of the average person's full-time earnings. For some parents the cost (especially if you include gas and, in many cases, the need for a second car) and the time involved actually outweigh what they might earn.

A positive development is day-care centers provided by employers at the workplace. For giving child and parent easy access—at coffee breaks and lunchtime, for meals, and in reducing travel time—this is a big improvement. Employers benefit too, from relaxed and happier staff.

Family Day Care

Family day care is a scheme by which local authorities license mothers in their own homes to care for up to five children from other families. Usually only one of these can be a baby; the others will be varied in age. Houses are inspected thoroughly for safety standards—child-safe cupboards, gates, fences, and so on. Family day-care coordinators are watchful that good care is being provided, and will not license a caregiver who is considered unsatisfactory.

When choosing a caregiver, the best bet is to look for someone who has been doing it for some time, and seems happy and well organized. Trust your own feelings around that person, and about that household, and look carefully at the demeanor of the children there.

The huge plus is that family day care is a home environment, and with luck, a stable relationship can form in which your child feels they are cared for as an individual. As with any trust relationship, time and getting to know a person are your only guides. If you are lucky, this person may become a family friend as well as a loving addition to your child's life.

Family day care is more personal than a child-care center for you, too. You can take the time to get to know your child's caregiver over a cup of coffee, and become friends as much as possible. It's fine to make a few inquiries and visit a few caregivers to see how you "click." This relationship is too important to leave to chance.

There is a small but important risk, in any child-care situation, of sexual abuse, perhaps by a husband or older boy or girl in a household, or by workers or visitors at a center. (Hospital studies have found that 10 percent of serious abuse takes place in a child-care setting.) One criterion for letting your child be cared for by others is that the child has reached an age where he or she can tell you clearly if something is wrong.

Preschools

Preschools are exactly what
the name suggests—a part-time
introduction to school life for
children aged around three to
five. Many parents find them
a great idea and decide when
their child should begin depending on the individual child's
readiness.

Preschools are a good child-care option for many parents.
Since they are an outgrowth of school rather than of the need
to have children looked after, they are more education-based
than most other centers. Preschools usually run only a half
day or short day session, and most children attend fewer
than five days a week. (It's noteworthy that educationists consider this enough time for young children to be in a structured
setting.)

Because of the short hours, preschools are ideal for at-home
parents, but are usually not convenient for employed parents
who need their children taken care of for longer hours.

Nannies

Nannies are at-home one-on-one caregivers chosen and
employed by you. This is obviously expensive, and quality is
hugely variable. (Do they watch your child, or your TV set?)
Nannying is a lonely job for someone who isn't really cut out
for it. On a popular national radio talk show, we once heard a
caller tell of her one-year-old son having had three nannies in
six months "Still," she said, "it's not much fun for seventeen-
year-old girls being with a baby all day." (Nor, we might add, is

this situation much fun for the baby.) On the plus side, some nannies are superb, and an enormous help to the family unit. And the child is cared for in your home.

There is a side effect to nannies that most parents will be aware of, since it applies to any good-quality care. Studies of nanny use in affluent North American families found that a good nanny actually damaged the child's relationship with its mother, since the child naturally gravitated to the person who provided the warmth and time. It's an understandable problem, but it is really a problem of overuse that could be avoided by balancing time with mother, father, and nanny. There is nothing wrong with loving lots of people.

Family and Friends

By far the greatest amount of child care used in the U.S. is still that provided by family and friends—grandparents, neighbors, and so on. This is especially favored by families of non-U.S. origin, where family and cultural ties tend to be particularly strong and supportive.

When family and friends are caring for children, the same precautions still need to be taken and care must be taken that arrangements are fair to all concerned. But by and large, children are loved and cared for because they are family, and this timeless way of sharing the joy and work of childr earing has a lot going for it.

◡◞ Discipline—A Problem Area ◞◡ for Caregivers

*T*HE PRESSURE on a caregiver is to avoid trouble— to sidestep the discipline wrangles that parents at home with kids must have, and from which children learn important lessons. Children who misbehave in care must be distracted, appeased, but not confronted (and we parents would not want caregivers to take such firm disciplinary action). It's the same with affection—it has to be diluted. Nap time is spent on a mat, not in an armchair in the arms of a loving relative. If caregivers wanted to give this amount of affection (and they often do), they would not have the time.

A child will often attract far more notice in child care if they present a problem. Aggressive children, or very upset children, get attended to. Well-behaved children may be invisible. Child-care caregivers have told us of the labeling syndrome, by which a child develops in the first few days an identity as a "problem child," when he or she may just have been having a tough time settling in. The "word" on who is being "a problem" is passed on—from shift to shift and then from year to year. This reputation can follow a child right through to school.

Parents approach their own child in a totally different way than the way they approach anyone else's. We talked to one day-care center director who sends her own child to another day-care center, because she felt it would be unfair to have him around when she is in her professional role. Another had the opposite policy—she wouldn't dream of having her child away from her.

We parents are intensely interested in our own child. Notice how you bore your friends with every detail of your child's progress. Look at it from the child's point of view. Might it not matter to children to spend their first two or three years among people who adore them, who long to see them learn and grow, and have a personal investment and pride in them? Although a paid worker may genuinely care about children's well-being and advancement, the best they can ever do is to be fond of your child, and be tender toward him or her in a general sort of way. What they have to offer will never equal a parent's investment and intensity.

◆

Quality Care Is Still Just Care

*T*HE MOST overused word in the child-care debate is "quality." Nobody is happy with the idea of bleak, overcrowded child-care centers with cold and cruel staff. But "quality" care is usually proposed as being equal to (or even, it is implied, better than) the care a parent can provide.

CARE ISN'T LOVE

The real question has to be whether children receive continuity of care, from individuals who have a long-term relationship with them, whom they come to trust and love.

Love is at the heart of the whole matter. It might be possible to improve the intimate connection children make with staff by addressing issues like staff rostering, size of groups, whether caregivers move through with the same group, and how many different adults are supposed to interact with a child during their time in care.

The debate about quality generally centers on training of staff, facilities, nutrition, and educational programs. All these are important, but they sidestep the question of quality relationships. Spending one's early childhood in the care of twenty or thirty different individuals (even in the best of settings) is still a very odd kind of childhood.

The use of the words "child care" is a great piece of marketing. We have to ask: is child care actually just "watching" children, or "educating" them, or is it "raising" them? If you spend eight or nine hours a day of infancy and toddlerhood in a day-care center, then these people are surely raising you. Yet no one in the child-care industry is proposing that professionals take over the primary role of the parents. It has somehow been assumed that parents will still provide all that is needed, even though parent-child contact time has shrunk, and shrunk, and shrunk. The development of intimacy skills in a child in care may not be happening at all. The child as a person may be falling through the cracks.

Child-care academics have high aims, but the reality is often different. Child-care students and new workers we interviewed often spoke of the huge gap between their college or university ideals of "individualized programs" and "one-to-one interaction," and the reality of

life in a busy center. Child care is a highly stressful occu-
pation—health problems, rapid turnover, and total
burnout in workers and directors are very common.

✦

WHAT IS THE BIG PICTURE?

TODAY THE UNITED States has a larger proportion of women in
the paid workforce than any other developed country. Women
make up 49 percent of our entire workforce, compared with
only 25 percent in Germany, 27 percent in England, 22 percent
in Ireland, 36 percent in Italy. In Europe there is far more gov-
ernmental support for parents who choose to take a few years
off work. For instance, in Sweden, the government pays 90 percent of your pre-baby income for one year, and either parent
can be the one to stay at home.

As a result, there are many varieties of American childhood.
Of the twenty-one million children aged five and under in the
U.S., almost a tenth, or two and half million, spend all day, five
days a week, in a day-care center. Far more—about twice this
number—attend day care but only part-time. Other forms of
care—relatives, friends, family home care—are used for about a
third of all children (seven million or so) for a significant part
of each week. And six and a half million, or one-third of all

American children, are still cared for primarily by their mother and/or father in their own home.

When you analyze the situation, it emerges that day care is actually the least-preferred choice of parents, especially for young babies. More than half of the people who use day care do not do so until their child is at least three years old. Immigrant and non-white minority parents, who are often the most economically stressed, strongly prefer to use relatives or family arrangements to care for their children, and many say they would find it extremely distressing to leave their babies in the care of strangers. This is even the case in countries where day care is free. Day care is culturally unacceptable to them.

Looking even closer at the figures, a further surprising finding occurs. If we stop looking at averages, and do what is called "disaggregating" the figures, to see if there are different trends hidden away, it emerges that there seem to be two distinct groups of parents, with totally different attitudes to day care. The largest group by far, which we could call the traditional parent group, wait as long as they can before returning to full-time work. This is regardless of income. Along with parents in Germany, England, and Australia, and most developed countries, there is a preference to stay home with babies and toddlers as long as possible, and use day care sparingly if at all. However, a small group—including a high proportion of very affluent parents as well as some under financial duress, place their babies into day care full-time *soon after they are born and send them there continually until they are of school age*. It's as if parents in this group want to have children, but not take a full-time role in raising them. This group, totaling about 800,000 babies, or one-fifth of all the under-one's, is still a minority, but its numbers have grown enormously in recent decades.

Whatever else you may conclude, you would have to say that this is a very different kind of childhood. And as we shall see from the best research available to date, far from an ideal one.

THE REAL PROBLEM—THE MOTHERHOOD GHETTO

THERE ARE TWO things that drive mothers back to work when they would rather be at home.

One is economic dependency. Depending on another person's income can make the parent at home feel vulnerable and depressed. The nonearning partner can be made to feel that her work is worthless since she is "just caring for kids."

Another reason is the fear of "going crazy"–being with small children for company all day. This is a real problem, but not exactly a child's fault. The problem lies in the whole way we live. Our suburbs and apartment blocks may look pleasant enough, but are often very lonely places. We live surrounded by strangers, and the only social life is a trip to the supermarket. It's possible, through community centers, play groups, churches, swimming clubs, and other organizations, to become more connected, and to bring about social change. But to do this, a person needs to be fairly confident and socially skilled.

It could be argued that Ethiopian farmers or Calcutta slum dwellers have a better life than Westerners in terms of social support and sheer friendliness of daily living.

REVITALIZING THE SUBURBS

IF MORE PARENTS were at home in the daytime, then things in the suburbs would soon change. You can already see this happening–play groups, community centers, and many other formal and informal networks of women and men are developing. Some of these will be oriented around children, others will be purely for self-development, or action groups for important issues like the environment, or more resources for families.

As men choose to be more family focused, and as more people work at home (thanks to computers) or work shorter hours, suburbs may change from deserted dormitories into lively and safe places where life goes on at its best.

Is This the Perfect Way to Live?

*O*N A wooded suburban ridge overlooking Hobart's harbor in Australia, a cluster of houses stands out only slightly from the conventional houses close by. They have warm, earthy colors, detailed woodwork in Tasmanian timbers. More noticeably—they have no road, only landscaped pathways and discreet parking bays at the edge of the three-acre site.

This is the Cascade Cohouse—a form of living for people of all ages that has been highly successful in northern Europe, and is now gaining a foothold in Australia. For a young family that has to live in the city, this may well be the perfect way to live.

THE SETUP

Cascade Cohouse consists of fifteen dwellings that run along a hillside, curving at one end to face a larger common building, which everyone shares the use of.

A large, attractive "village square" is at the center and a pedestrian pathway curves amid gardens and terraces. On completion of the Cohouse, thirty to forty people will live here. They will each own their unit just as in any apartment complex. Each dwelling fronts onto common pedestrian space, but has a private back yard.

Best of all, all occupants will share in the large common building with dining room for forty people, children's playroom, well-equipped workshop, meditation spaces, office space, and kitchens. Occupants may either interact and join with other people on a daily basis or be entirely private, since the houses are quite self-contained.

This isn't a commune, yet it is a real community. One of the nicest parts of Cohouse living is that a shared evening meal system exists. Each adult member is scheduled to cook a meal for the community from time to time. At present that means once every eight weeks— it's your turn! Eventually these meals will be held four evenings a week. For a young working father or mother, this means that instead of arriving home from work and scraping a meal together for the family, one can often simply stroll over to the Commonhouse for a delicious prepared dinner.

A SAFE PLACE FOR CHILDREN TO GROW

Ian and Jane, two young scientists who were founding members of the Cohouse, explained why the Cohouse situation was ideal for them as parents of a two-year-old child. They could, if they wished, go out two or three nights a week and have excellent baby-sitting available. Their little girl could walk to the houses of her young friends or older members of the Cohouse who enjoyed having young ones around. Since this was a group of people who knew each other and chose to live in community, the feeling of trust and companionship was everywhere.

Young mothers or fathers at home during the day had company for a chat simply by strolling outside or going to the Commonhouse. There was also an apartment for visitors of residents.

Older people felt secure and never lonely—although privacy was not only respected but designed into the buildings.

INEXPENSIVE LIVING

As for costs, the residents at Cascade Cohouse found that they could build a very attractive dwelling of 1000 to 1200 square feet for $70,000. Purchasing strata title and common ownership of facilities—including the thirty square Commonhouse—cost an additional $32,000. This included all hidden costs such as service connection and stamp duty (which normally add over $8,000 to the cost of a suburban block).

(These are Australian dollars, which are equivalent to only about fifty cents U.S. So if you double these figures you will get an idea of what it costs to live in this Australian cohouse—which is sadly now fully occupied. The main point is that cohousing is less expensive than a single-family dwelling, as it uses much less land and utilities, yet offers many more amenities through the sharing of facilities.)

Cohouses provide many qualities in living that simply cannot be bought—companionship, safety, meals, low travel costs, solar design, and all kinds of sharing potential. Some cohouses in Europe have shared ownership in vacation homes and yachts at the coast, and have their own swimming pool or sauna.

To read more about cohouses, try the excellent book *Cohousing—A Contemporary Approach to Housing Ourselves* by Kathryn McCammant (Ten Speed Press).

‿⋮ Conflicting Views—The ∿ Experts Slug It Out

"**POOR QUALITY** care in these years can sometimes harm young children. Leaving babies and toddlers unattended and unoccupied for long periods, inappropriate discipline, lack of a good planned program or even leaving a distressed child uncomforted can make childcare an unhappy experience for parents and children alike."

—Australian Labor Policy Statement,
1993 Federal election

"**I'VE NEVER** advised mothers who wanted a career not to pursue it, but I think it's very cruel for mothers who would rather stay at home to have to turn their kids over to someone else. If a mother wants to stay home with her baby, the government should subsidize her, as in most other Western countries."

—Benjamin Spock, the *Mercury*, November 1992

"**FROM MY** experience, childcare (if carefully chosen) is not just good for children, they thrive on it! They benefit from a rich, stimulating environment away from the narrowness of an exclusive relationship with one parent. They have a larger view of the world and learn to share and cooperate with one another. They spend time with adults who enjoy being with them, and zoom in on their needs day after day. They are creative, self reliant and, I suspect, appreciate their parents a little more because their time together is so special."

—Rosemary Lever, *Such Sweet Sorrow*

"**QUALITY CARE** is hard to come by, and even if you are one of the lucky ones, once your children are in care your life will entail a daily round of juggling childcare pickups and daily duties. If you're anything like me you will also have to live with a mixture of feelings and impossible contradictions, swinging between joy, happiness, or gloomy questioning about whether the care you have chosen is suitable, whether the children are happy, whether they're getting enough time and attention from you."

—Rosemary Lever, *Such Sweet Sorrow*

"**THE FACT** is that the children of good, working parents are just as happy and turn out equally well as those of parents who don't work. It is not quantity of time you spend with your child that counts, it is the quality."

—Christopher Green, *Toddler Taming*

"**REGULAR ABSENCES** can be damaging for children under three. Only from ages three to six, can most children profit from a whole day in high quality group care. But even then, there is a consensus among preschool educators that the benefits of a good preschool program diminish or are even cancelled when the school day is prolonged to six hours or beyond."

—Selma Fraiberg, child psychoanalyst,
quoted by Karl Zinsmeister in "Hard Truths About
Day Care," *Reader's Digest*, January 1989

" . . . **INFANTS** in day care are more likely to develop insecure attachments to their mothers, withdrawal from their mothers, and were more likely to hit, kick, threaten, and argue, than those who were not in day care or started later."

"Children with a record of early non-parental care show more serious aggression, less cooperation, less tolerance of frustration, more misbehavior, and at times social withdrawal.

—Karl Zinsmeister, "Hard Truths About Day Care,"
Reader's Digest, January 1989

" . . . THE point is that day care was introduced for the adult's benefit and investigations into whether or not it is helpful or damaging for the child come later. Day care is about adult economics, adult behavior, and adult desires."

—Bob Mullen, *Are Mothers Really Necessary?*

"BRUNER (1980) concludes that in its present form, child-minding creates problems for at least a third of the children in such care, and for possibly as many as half."

—Bob Mullen, *Are Mothers Really Necessary?*

"SHEILA KITZINGER notes that the social context of child-bearing has become negative and rejecting—childbearing is an interruption of people's 'real' lives. Kitzinger adds that this particular ethos which downgrades motherhood and childrearing, attributes to those mothers who find motherhood satisfying a mindless, sentimental form of idiocy. Kitzinger believes that in the women's movement, whatever that might be, there is an ambiguous approach to motherhood."

—Bob Mullen, *Are Mothers Really Necessary?*

"FIRST-TIME parents are often unprepared for the intensity of love they have for their children. One mother I met recently described it as being "metamorphosed." She held a senior position in a large banking firm and had committed herself while pregnant to an early return date. The day we met she marveled about how changed she felt by the birth of her child, how privileged, how much more love she had to give and how painful it was even to contemplate leaving her precious baby with any-one else."

—Rosemary Lever, *Such Sweet Sorrow*

"**SOMEHOW I** have rationalized the horrible fact that an unskilled shop assistant earns more than twice the money of a child-care worker, but that the accountant setting up our new television company sent a bill of $150 an hour for his expert consultation and advice.

"Nevertheless I felt sick in the stomach after handing over $10 to the beautiful human being who'd cared for my son that day. I still feel sick."

—Kirsty Cockburn, *ITA*, October 1989

◆

TOO, TOO, TOO

Child care is here to stay. What we have to guard against is child-care overuse. Our standards have somehow slipped. We have been sucked in by economic rationalism, and stopped listening to our own hearts.

The result—children are being put into care too young, for too many hours, too many days a week.

The inadequate provision of child care means that parents are having to use too many different forms of care, even in the same day, to meet their needs.

Child-care workers are paid too little, and there are too many children. Center-based care is too unnatural and mech-anistic a form of looking after young children, too factory-like for comfort.

In the future, there will be a place for child care, but it will be a smaller place than it now occupies. While everyone talks about the need for more child-care places and bemoans the waiting lists, it may be that one day there will be less demand for it, and places will be abundant for those who really need it. Little babies and toddlers will mainly be cared for once again where they have been for millennia—by their parents, neighbors, and family members, in the arms and in the homes of those who love them.

RECOMMENDATIONS

THE CHOICES WE make about child care should be based firstly on the developmental needs of our child.

As mentioned earlier in this chapter, there are no conclusive research results that set down what is right for every child. We parents have to use our own good sense. The following are guidelines I recommend.

By Age

In your child's first year, do not use institutional child care at all.

Arrange for your baby to be with one of you all the time, except for occasional breaks—days off or evenings out, when you have a trusted and familiar baby-sitter.

If you are using institutional child care, we suggest you consider these guidelines:

When the child is one: up to one short day per week, for example, 10 A.M. to 3 P.M.

When the child is two: up to two short days per week.

When the child is three: up to three short days or half-days a week.

When the child is four: up to four short days or half-days a week.

Your decisions should always be based on the needs of the individual child, and through monitoring his or her reactions from day to day.

By Type of Care

In order of preference, we believe the best source of child care for your child under the age of three would be:

*** Close relative or friend whom you trust and who loves your child.

** A trustworthy and friendly family day care caregiver, whom you know personally. If you cannot find a family day care you are really comfortable with, then a child-care center is probably better.

* A quality child-care center, with stable staff whom you get to know and feel comfortable with.

For children three years and older, good child-care centers can come into their own. At this age, the benefits of social interaction, planned activities, playing space and equipment, and professionally trained and motivated staff are a major bonus.

By Your Circumstances

As well as the needs of the child, the needs of the family unit must be weighed in—because the child will suffer anyway if, for instance, a parent becomes sick, or a marriage breaks down, or a family cannot keep its home through lack of income.

If child care is truly good for your family, it will be filling the following criteria:

1. It helps your survival—for instance, when you need to work to provide for material needs.
2. It gives you time to care adequately for other children, for example a new baby or a sick child.
3. It provides things for your child that you can't provide—resources (if poor), stimulation (if limited at home), friends (if isolated or an only child).
4. It meets your standards for discipline, respect for the child, and safety.
5. It builds long-term relationships—caregivers become your friends, and friends of your child.
6. It is a setting where you feel welcome to drop in at any time, spend the day with your child, make special requests, or let them know of concerns, without ever feeling you are a bother.

By balancing a child's needs and your changing family situation, informed choices can be made that may work out very well.

Good luck!

∿ **five** ∿

Raising Boys

IT'S TIME THAT WE PLAN

FOR A NEW KIND OF MAN

✦

If YOU HAVE a daughter, then things are looking up for her. Because of the gains women have struggled for and won in the last few decades, your daughter will have as much chance of being a doctor as of being a nurse, a boss as a secretary. She will have the right to equal pay, the right to leave a violent husband, and the means to do so. Nobody will own her.

But there is still a long way to go. Your daughter will not have the freedom to walk about at night. In her life she will meet all kinds of barriers caused by men's inner insecurities. She may have trouble finding a man to settle down with who is as emotionally healthy as she is. Clearly, in the progress we are making through feminism, there's a missing step—something still has to happen with men to bring them along on the journey to freedom that women are making. We can make a big difference if we start early, with boys.

GIVING BOYS A POSITIVE SELF-IMAGE

THINK ABOUT THE present situation of boys. If you hear on the radio about a gang of youths causing a fight, you're pretty sure it will be boys, not girls. When we talk about teenage suicide, in four out of five cases we mean boys. The driver of a crashed car, the cause of a high-speed chase, the problem child in the classroom or playground, the burglar, the serial killer, the corporate criminal, the dictator—why is it almost always a male?

> *Boys have five times as many learning problems, display ten times as much problem behavior at school. As adults they will have four times the vehicle accident rate and nine times the imprisonment rate of women.*

If you have boy children, it isn't enough to let them grow up to be "normal"—because normal for a man in today's world often means uptight, competitive, and emotionally illiterate. It's time to start raising a "new kind of man."

This chapter is about realizing just how much more we can expect of boys if we are willing to expand our horizons for them.

The first step for us as parents is to get a clear idea of the kind of men we want our sons to be.

What Kind of Man Do We Need?

A GROUP OF women is meeting in a weekend seminar on relationships. (In another room, the men who are their partners are also meeting.) The leader asks the women to call out the qualities they look for in a man. After the quick rush of jokes like "Lots of money," and some unprintable comments, the women become more thoughtful. This is the list that they come up with.

Passionate

Self-reliant

Willing to share the work

Able to love deeply

Able to feel sorrow and admit fear, and not just turn everything into anger

Respectful to and supportive of women

Nurturing

Fearless and strong in good causes

Creative—not rigid or bound by convention

Respectful of others

Funny, but knows when to be serious

Stable, reliable (but not dull)

Sticks to a task, gets things done

Loving, but not gooey or dependent

Proud, but not egotistical

Safe and not violent

Able to dance and sing and smell the roses

Not just a workaholic

Wild and free

Impulsive

Natural

These are the qualities women look for in a man. It's a fairly safe bet that this is also what men want to be themselves.

So when we are raising our sons, these can be some of the aims we have in mind. This awareness will guide our actions and help us know when to intervene in the smallest of everyday situations. When a boy is mean to his sister, or tickles her when she is clearly saying no—then as parents we come in very firmly and tell him not to do that. We would do just the same if she was mean to him. If he asks why, we tell him, "I want you to grow up respecting people's bodies, and respecting your own too. When someone says stop, you stop." You can see how important this is for a lifetime.

HOW THE WORLD TREATS BOYS

THERE'S SOMETHING SPECIAL and precious about boys—every parent of boys and girls notices that their natures are different. Boys tend to wear their feelings on their sleeves—often their passions are strong and they seem to have an urge to protect. They love heroism and action. Boys are loyal, stoic, and have a strong sense of justice. They are humorous, optimistic, and up-front.

When I look at little boys, and then see how cheaply the world often treats them—how few of their special qualities are supported and nurtured—it makes me very sad.

There are some stunning facts that sum up the situation of boys today.

The first is the bottom line—survival. A boy is three times more likely to die before his twenty-first birthday than a girl—largely from preventable causes—accident, violence, suicide, drug overdose. He is nine times more likely to end up in prison. Nine times more likely to get expelled or suspended from school. Three times more likely to have learning disabilities or be in a remedial class.

Another, separate piece of information, which researchers now believe is closely linked to the above problems, is that the average father spends about six minutes a day in interaction with his children. So while boys and girls both get less fathering than at any time in history (especially when we add the effects of family breakdown and families without fathers), this is especially a problem for boys because fathers are their main source of information on how to be a man. So it's time we looked more closely at what we can do to help boys turn out well.

We'll sum up what is needed, then go into each issue more fully.

1. Boys need fathers, or at least very good father substitutes.
2. Fathers need help from other men to raise their sons.
3. Boys need to learn how to behave around girls—respecting them, being equal to them.
4. Boys need protection from being cheapened, hardened, or debased by exposure to violence or banality. They need to see their sexuality as special, not cheap.
5. Boys need help to learn how to work and be self-sufficient around the house.

WHERE HAVE ALL THE FATHERS GONE?

ONE HUNDRED AND fifty years ago, life was very different for men and boys. Almost all men worked in agriculture and home-based crafts and trades. So a boy grew up around his dad and the other men of the village or town; his uncles, cousins, grandparents all took an interest in teaching him and befriending him. Then suddenly, when the industrial revolution began, whole villages were evicted and millions of people went to the cities and towns to work in the mills and mines. Mothers had the task of raising their sons, as the fathers were away at work six days a week for long hours. "Wait till your father gets home!" became a common refrain.

Losing the support of the village network, the family itself started to decline. A hundred years ago, an average family had

6.7 children. Few people we know want to go back to that! But families didn't just get smaller. They started to fall apart. Men left their wives, or never married in the first place. Soon a large number of children were being raised by single women. This trend has continued to the present day. Men are disappearing from the family picture. For instance, within a year of divorce, one-third of fathers have virtually disappeared from their children's lives.

A father can be around and still have "disappeared" emotionally. Many working men are out of the house early, home late, and tired and irritable when they are at home. Little children may not see their father at all during the week—they are asleep when he leaves in the morning and again when he comes home at night. An unemployed father, if he gets his act together, has a better chance of being a good father than someone with a busy career.

Father absence hurts and damages little girls too, but it devastates little boys. Whether they show it by being aggressive, or compensate by being Mommy's little helper, a boy with no role models cannot learn how to be a man. Some psychologists believe it may take hours per day of male contact for a boy to learn how to be a man. If little David has a lady schoolteacher, lives with his mom, stays at Grandma's, and meets only Mom's women friends at home, he learns nothing about how to be a man. The absence of men in boys' lives is a big problem in our society.

WHAT CAN YOU DO IF YOU'RE A SINGLE MOM?

WOMEN ON THEIR own can raise healthy sons. But as I've learned from talking to lots of single mothers, it takes some special planning.

Being Firm, Staying Warm

A single parent of either sex continually has to switch between and balance the firmlove and softlove sides of his or her nature. For a single mother, there will be a danger of losing the softness while trying to maintain the firmness you know your son needs. As a rule, women are less combative than men in their interaction style. You can see this in the way some men say things like, "Not you again!" "What's up, man?" and so on in their friendly greetings. Discipline generally comes more easily for a father than a mother. In fact, sometimes while a mother is trying to be firmer, her partner is trying to tone down his hardness and be more reasonable.

There are times when boys (mostly unconsciously) seek out a combative (friendly, safe, but very confronting) intensity to help them deal with their physical and hormonal surges. Get help–from friends, or professionally–if you feel you are losing the control here. Especially with boys around fourteen years of age, a mother on her own needs to conserve energy and be well supported. It's especially important never to hit or strike, or say hurtful kinds of things at these times.

Why Boys Misbehave

*M*ARCUS IS fourteen. He likes to go off in the evenings on his bike and hang around with his friends. One night, he's late for dinner. When he comes in his parents grumble and nag at him, but his father is only half-hearted about it. In the end, it's agreed that Marcus can come in when he pleases as long as he's in by dark, and that his dinner will be left in the oven.

A few weeks later Marcus comes in really late, about nine o'clock. He says it wasn't really dark. His mother is upset, but his father says—well, as long as he doesn't get into any serious trouble, and is in by ten. Boys like to have a little freedom.

A few days later, Marcus is brought home by the police, who found him with CDs stolen from a nearby mall. He is one of a group of boys to be charged with the offense.

Marcus's parents, especially his father, wanted to avoid trouble. But they missed the point that Marcus was breaking the rules to get noticed. When the rules were just bent to give him more scope, he had to break even bigger rules. Marcus's father is a senior manager, and has been away overseas a lot. An intelligent man, he will now make the connection, and start to do some fathering. Marcus will be confronted about his behavior, but more importantly, his father will get more involved. A promotion involving extra travel will be turned down so that he can be at home more of the time. It will cost him materially, but Marcus will stay out of jail.

Boys misbehave because they want to be "met" by an equal investment of energy, preferably from fathers or father substitutes. Boys whose fathers are uninvolved are especially drawn to "hypermasculine" action figures, comics, and games. They are trying to make up for the lack of masculinity in their real lives. Boys with involved fathers are noticeably quieter, more communicative, and more settled. They achieve more at school, have fewer behavior problems, and are more often employed when they leave school.

Studies have found the incidence of drug addiction and alcoholism in boys is directly proportionate to the amount of time spent with parents. Adolescence is not a time to ignore your children.

✦

Finding the Right Role Models

You must actively look for role models for your son. Go down to the school and ask the principal for a good male teacher for your son next year. When choosing a sport or activity, choose it by looking at the kind of men who lead the activity. Is this the kind of man I want my son to be like? (That is what role model means. Looked at this way, the football coach or karate teacher could be great, or the pits!)

Sometimes an uncle or grandfather will take an interest if you ask them to do so—they may have been holding back because they were unsure if their help was welcome. You don't have to marry someone to get a good role model.

Be very, very choosy about whom your son spends time with. Pedophiles (men who sexually abuse children) often take advantage of boys with no fathers who are hungry for male attention. This isn't a rare problem—one in seven boys is abused at some time in his childhood. Always check out the men in your son's life.

Send Him to His Dad

Unless your son's father is a dangerous or very irresponsible man, do your best to maintain contact between them. If you are separated or divorced, but in good communication with your ex-husband, consider sending your son to live with his dad from the time the boy is about fourteen years old. Often boys get difficult to manage around fourteen. Without realizing it, they feel a strong need for male limit-setting. Women often fear taking this step—"Oh, he wouldn't take good care of him!" Sometimes this is true. But more often fathers, if called upon to take on the parenting, will find that they have untapped nurturing and disciplining qualities. This arrangement can work out well for everyone.

Single parenting is heroic work. It's better to be a child in a single-parent home than in a bitterly unhappy intact family. The challenge for single parents is to supplement your own parenting with the right inputs for your kids.

WHAT FATHERING REALLY MEANS

MANY DADS ARE great with their kids. However, many of us are completely at a loss regarding "how to father." Early in my children's lives I found it tempting to just leave parenting to my wife because she seemed so much better at it. Today, though, fathering is one of the biggest pleasures of my life.

Part of the reason for our incompetence is that we have a fathering vacuum—many men didn't have an involved father, just a strange man who shuffled newspapers in the corner of the living room and grumbled occasionally. So we didn't have a deep pool of fathering behaviors to draw from.

Luckily I can say to you from experience, "It ain't that hard," and "Once you get started you'll soon get to like it." Here are two or three good ways to start.

Rough and Tumble

Boys love to wrestle, tickle, struggle, and play in vigorous, rough-housing ways. This seems to be true at any age. Do this whenever you get the chance and have the energy. Choose a safe place. Give them a goal–to pin your arms, or escape from a bear hug.

There is more to it than just good fun–you can teach important lessons while you wrestle. By stopping if it gets too careless or dangerous, calming down, and beginning again, you are teaching boys to handle and be calm with their strength. By always being good-humored and not excessively competitive–letting them win, then winning again–you teach them that the fun is in the interaction, and to be good losers. Perhaps most importantly, play wrestling, or "rough and tumble," is both a form of intimacy and a celebration of masculinity. (Though some daughters like it too, especially when they are little.)

My own father was not into hugging or outward displays of affection, and like many men of his generation, couldn't give a compliment to save his life. But he would always play wrestle with me, with my cousins, and with nephews. Whenever we went visiting, he would be covered with kids. It was great!

Doing and Teaching

Robert Bly says, "Even mean men are sweet when they teach." Boys love to learn about the world of men. This might mean cars, computers, horses, birdwatching, fishing, woodwork–anything that they enjoy, and you enjoy showing them. (A tip–don't be perfectionist, or you'll just put them off. Share your enjoyment, not just your high standards.)

If you're a dad, you should be around your son and the rest of the family, talking and doing things, for at least an hour a day. If your work schedule prevents this, you might need to look seriously at your priorities. I would like to be more comforting about this, but being a career success today is almost incompatible with being a good father. Boys need to know you in all different moods and different activities.

Listen Up!

O NE OF the greatest life skills you can ever have is the ability—the willingness, really—to stop in the middle of an argument and listen to the other person's side of the story. It's a skill you could use at least five times a day . . .

One hot summer afternoon my son and I went down the gully to start the diesel pump. We do this once every summer to refill our dam with water. My son was four— a little young you might say, but a necessary assistant. While I cranked the pump, his job was to flick the pressure switch at the critical moment for the pump to start.

The machine is huge and old, and we had several failed attempts. I was not in a good mood. Thistles stung my legs, and mosquitoes swirled around. My arm ached from turning the heavy crank. Then my assistant went on strike! He backed off around the dam! I could feel my anger rise. I prepared myself to bully him into doing as he was told. But he looked me squarely in the eyes, accusing me almost, and I managed to catch myself. "Why won't you help?" I asked, trying to make my voice sympathetic. "It's too smoky. I can't breathe," he said. Sure enough, a pall of diesel fumes hung around from our first attempts.

So we sat by the water for a few minutes, quietly relaxing before trying again. We chatted a little about the frogs and the insects. Then we started the pump the first time!

It hasn't been the last time, and probably the experience gets more frequent as children get older and wiser. That moment of simple parental realization—"They're right and I'm wrong." And how important it is to listen.

✦

Seeing You in Action

If sons see you cooking meals, cleaning up, and caring for younger kids, then they will also become more hardworking around the home. Dads have to show they are more than just "the good-times man." You can teach them by example how to be whole men. If they see you taking care of your body, treating other people well, expressing your emotions, standing up for what you believe in, then this will be more powerful than anything you might say. You might just have to become the kind of man you want your sons to be!

Let Your Son Meet Other Men

Involve your sons in activities with your friends so they can meet, learn from, and get the approval of other men. Go on fathers-and-sons camping trips. Take your sons to work so that they see from time to time what you do with your life—where you fit into the big picture, what your ideals are. Let them see some of what you sacrifice, some of the hardship and endurance that your life involves.

Above all, be around for them. Have time to waste.

BOYS NEED PROTECTION

I WAS ONCE waiting outside an elementary school for a meeting at the end of the school day. A group of boys—grade three, eight-year-olds—were coming slowly out of the classroom. Seeing something wasn't quite right, I looked more closely. Several were wiping tears from their eyes. All looked pale, shocked. I discovered later from a parent that their teacher—a man—had just shown an R-rated war video because it was Memorial Day. No discussion, no debriefing, no breaks—just ninety minutes of violence. Often men and boys get blamed for being unfeeling, aggressive, insensitive. But how do they become that way, except as a defense against what we assail them with?

You can do a lot to slow down the robbing of childhood from your sons (and daughters) by preventing them from watching endless violent cartoons or playing unimaginative games with war toys. (Kids do make guns from sticks, yes, but all you can do with a toy gun is pretend to kill.) Much war and violent play arises from watching violence, feeling frightened by it, and so identifying with the war figures to get back a sense of power. Children in war zones play the most war games. Why should our living rooms resemble war zones? Why not have a home (and a TV environment) that brings in the feeling of a tropical island paradise, with nature, warmth, beauty, and adventure?

It's the same with computers. Don't let your sons "disappear" into banal computer games for hours on end—especially the kind with endless mazes and ladders, which are addictive and teach nothing but a twitchy finger.

Provide more active, sociable, and natural kinds of activity. Spend time with your sons rather than buying things for them. Value and compliment their ability with little children, and their sensitivity to feelings and fairness. Have a pet that they can be active with. Do this and you will see the natural lovingness come out in your boys.

BOYS NEED HELP IN LEARNING TO RELATE

ONE GOOD THING that a mother or father of boys can do is to teach them to get along with the opposite sex, and help them to talk to and cooperate with girls. Insist they treat girls with respect and care. When they become teenagers, don't let them put pictures from girlie magazines on their walls. Most boys are interested in women's bodies, but you can help to keep sex and sexuality special and not just sleazy and cheap.

TEACH YOUR SON TO RESPECT WOMEN

AS A DAD, you do this in two ways—by showing respect to women yourself, and by coming down hard on any disrespect that is shown by a son to his mother. An old saying, "Don't speak to your mother like that," sets the scene for an important moment in family life. It should only need to be said once.

As a mom, calmly and clearly demand respect. Mediate with your son and his sisters so that they are able to express their feelings, and to learn respectful problem solving instead of name calling and intimidation. Be evenhanded. Boys have feelings—remember this yourself, and teach your daughters this. If boys are treated as though they have no feelings, then they become unfeeling to protect themselves.

Ask your son about his feelings and acknowledge when he is sad or scared. Let him know when you have these feelings too. Avoid the emotional shutdown that makes men so stressed and depressed. Don't ever make fun of his soft side, especially his early love life. He can be strong *and* sensitive. They go together.

HELP HIM LEARN HOUSEWORK SKILLS

AND PRAISE THOSE skills! By age nine, a son should be cooking a meal for the family each week and feeling proud of it. Even if it's only pasta and ready-made sauce to begin with, he can soon build up a creditable menu. Help him to get started in the kitchen. Most boys will gain enjoyment from making such a contribution.

Make it routine that he picks up after himself, learns to do laundry, and to sew. If he doesn't, don't nag—just double his workload for that day. The common response from SuperMom types is, "But it's quicker if I do it for him—he just takes so long." Yes, teaching takes time. But imagine having an eighteen-year-old who is as competent as you are, and who does as much housework as you do. Surely that's worth a little early investment!

IN SHORT

You are making a man. Think about the goals you have achieved, and those you still want to achieve. You could tick off on the list given by the women in the class at the start of this chapter. Which do you still want to work on?

At the very least, take time to have a dream about the kind of man you want your son to be. By making a commitment— "My sons will turn into wonderful young men"—and starting to do the daily things that make this happen you can, as a mother or father, achieve one of life's greatest satisfactions, and do the world a favor.

❧ **six** ❧

Raising Daughters

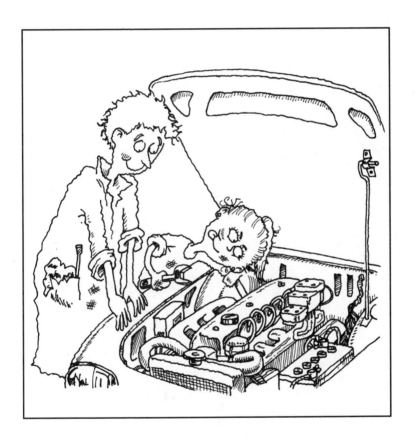

◆

Through HER DAUGHTER, a mother sees her own life starting again. So a daughter has a powerful effect on her mother. And how a mother feels about her own life will deeply influence how she relates to her daughter.

MOTHERS AND DAUGHTERS

MOTHERS AND DAUGHTERS can have a closeness that is very beautiful. Or they can be an explosive combination! Moms and daughters usually understand each other deeply–sometimes to an extent that seems telepathic.

Mothers feel so strongly about their daughters, just as fathers do about their sons, because in a sense our children are a new version of us. They reflect back to us all our hopes, fears, and feelings about our own lives. If you know this is going on, it helps. If you don't, it can lead to very weird behavior! Things can get fiery, as our teenagers become especially sensitive to being loaded up with our expectations. Such situations have led more than one mother to tell me she prefers sons—they're so much simpler!

But it's worth it. Part of what makes raising a daughter so great an adventure for a mother is the potential for close friendship. In the meantime, though, your daughter is a little child needing your care. To care for her well, you may have to work free of some of your own hang-ups that could be getting in the way of clear parenting.

What do we mean by this? Let's expand.

Mothers see themselves in their daughters. For better or for worse, this generates all kinds of unconscious and conscious urges.

+ They want their daughters to have more opportunities than they had.
+ They want their daughters to stay close, but also to move out and have their own lives.
+ They want their daughters to get along with their dads.
+ They want their daughters to find a man—as long as he's perfect!
+ They want their daughters to have a life free from pain or trouble of any kind.

What do we mean by unconscious urges? Here's an example: A friend of mine had a mother who had known great poverty in her childhood. Her idea of good mothering was working long hours so that her daughters would be well provided for. The result was that her daughters had very little time with her, and were often placed in vulnerable situations while their mother was away at work. They would have been better off with less money and more protection.

Sometimes when our motivation is unconscious like this, we don't think through all the ramifications. The key to this is self-awareness. You listen to what comes out of your own mouth, and reflect on "where you are coming from." You realize that your daughters are not you, and give them room to make their own mistakes, find their own answers, define what they want.

THE FIVE WAYS OF PARENTING

JEAN ILLSLEY CLARKE, in a superb book called *Growing Up Again*, describes five different ways we can react to a child, which also tell us a great deal about ourselves. You can use these five styles as a diagnostic tool to find what is happening between you and your daughter. Most probably, you'll find confirmation that you are doing the right thing, which Clarke calls the "assertively caring" style. The other styles can easily be recognized and help you to avoid doing harm.

When I first learned about these ideas (and this is talking as a dad) I found I was a real mixture of the different types. It was very helpful to think about.

It's also important to say here that none of these comments applies only to moms and daughters, but simply that being the same gender adds all kinds of intensity to the relationship. It can bring out mirroring tendencies where you see yourself in your offspring. Also, moms generally do more of the parenting. We understand more about mothers and daughters because they tend to express themselves more often and more clearly. And most mothers are ready and eager to change.

Let's apply the five styles to a simple everyday situation: Merrilee, a little girl aged six, falls over while running in the park. She comes to her mother crying, with a badly scraped arm.

There are several ways her mother can react.

The Abusive Style

Her mother is busy talking to a friend. She turns and yells, "Stop howling like that, or I'll really give you something to cry about." As she does so, she yanks the little girl by the arm and takes her home.

The message sent here is, "You don't count. Your feelings don't matter. You're a nuisance to me."

The child may feel deep pain and despair, or rage, or loneliness and withdrawal. But where is the mom coming from? If we're honest, many of us have felt overwhelmed at times, and reacted in a verbally abusive way. It's the reaction of a parent whose own needs are so unmet that she sees her daughter as a competitor.

This mother needs help of a nurturing, long-term kind so that she can refill her emotional fuel tank, heal her own childhood neglect, and in the meantime care for her daughter with more kindness.

The Conditional Style

This mother says, "Stop crying or I won't bandage your arm. What did you do that for anyway?" This kind of parent connects with the child by threats and conditions. The child has to meet with parental expectations, and only then will her needs be met. The message is, "Don't believe you are loveable; you only get love if you earn it."

The mother sends this message to her daughter because it's how she also views herself. This kind of parent is usually immaculate and uptight, setting super-high standards for herself and those around her. It's natural she will pass on the same messages to her child—especially if the child is the same sex as herself.

The child will feel inadequate, never quite measuring up—since no one is ever perfect. The child is likely to grow up obsessive and over-achieving, perhaps anorexic, with a lot of trouble being close to other people. In adulthood, she may have a series of showy but short-lived marriages.

The conditional mom needs to relax. She has to learn to find—and to give herself—love and approval just for being. She can learn to stop worrying so much about clothes, looks, money, or achievement. She should find some friends who are happy slobs, and learn how it's done. In this way she can learn to accept that love is free, and doesn't have to be earned. And then she can teach this to her children.

The Indulgent Style

Mommy rushes to the child before the little one has even had time to stand up. "Oh, look at your arm. That really hurts, doesn't it? I'll bandage it now. We'll drive to the pharmacy and get some ointment. I'll make you a bed on the couch in front of the TV and I'll do your jobs for you."

This sounds at first like a very kind mother. But listen to the deeper messages: "You are a poor victim. You aren't capable—you need me to look after you." At an even deeper level she is implying, "We can't both meet our needs at the same time. I'll overindulge you, but you'll owe me." Does this sound familiar to you?

The child in this relationship will have very mixed feelings. She will feel temporary comfort, but also a sense of obligation and resentment underlying it. She will feel weakened and confused by her parent's presence, rather than strengthened and encouraged. Jean Illsley Clarke calls this "a sticky, patronizing kind of love" that promotes dependency and a blurry sense of self.

The mother in this situation needs to build a stronger sense of self. Perhaps her childhood featured an alcoholic or otherwise needy parent who forced her to grow up too soon, and to be a caretaker instead of being loved. Perhaps one of her parents was also indulgent to mask inner neediness. She could benefit from reading books about codependency and getting good support in a healing kind of ongoing group.

The Neglectful Style

Mom ignores the scrape. In fact, she's probably not even at the playground. The daughter is blocks away from home, unsupervised, and nobody cares. This child may be fed and clothed, but her parents are uninvolved. She knows deep down that she dies or survives alone. If she has made it this far she will probably survive, but she is likely to be a very hard, lonely young person with all kinds of anger and disappointment hidden on the inside. She will possibly get into serious trouble in an attempt to get cared for. As an adult she will have little ability to get close to others unless help—in the form of an understanding teacher or youth worker—comes along soon.

Neglect is abuse, too—in some ways, one of the worst forms.

Before you get totally depressed, we'd better talk about the fifth kind of parenting style.

The Assertively Caring Style

This mother gives the little girl with the scraped arm a hug and loving care. She says things like, "Your arm is scraped. I'm sorry you are hurt. How about I clean it up for you?" And then, "How is it now?"

The child knows that she and her feelings matter. The mother is willing and available to help. Help is offered, not forced. The child feels comforted and relieved, secure, safe, and loved.

There's more, too, in the big picture. This kind of mother lets her child grow in independence. If the child is only slightly hurt, or is somewhat older, the mother leaves her in charge of what happens. She says things like, "Does it hurt? Are you able to go and wash it, or do you need some help?" This parent is available to give a hug, but is not too pushy. The message sent here is—"I trust you to make your own judgments about what you need" (and also, I don't need to be needed).

The assertively caring style is clearly the one to aim for.

When a Child Is Disabled

$\mathcal{I}$N ALL of my books on family life, it's been a concern to me that I have nothing to say about parenting disabled children. Yet every time I go on tour, parents of babies with all kinds of difficulties come along for some possible assistance. Children with disabilities are part of the family and the community, and deserve to be included. As much as anyone else, they are a plus in all our lives.

I've always felt constrained through lack of personal experience. So I was delighted when I found a beautiful article in the *Melbourne Age* by a mother of a daughter who is severely intellectually disabled, who can write about her child's life so far with real insight.

Mary Burbridge would be the first to say that her family life has had as many ups and downs as any other. However, it's clear to me that she has triumphed in all kinds of ways and that this would be the kind of message that other parents would like to hear. It is also an example of a very special relationship between a mother and her daughter.

MY DAUGHTER, MY FOREVER BABY

I have a darling baby. A patient, placid baby who nuzzles warmly into her sheepskin and gives me a sleepy smile when I come in. She sits up, bounces happily, and reaches up for a cuddle. I lift her out of bed, and with both hands held, she walks unsteadily to the bathroom to have her diaper changed.

She's at a delightful stage, liking to help with dressing and undressing, wanting to hold the spoon but making an awful mess, moving along on the furniture and pulling down whatever she can reach. She loves music—songs and rhymes sung to her, banging on the piano, clapping and finger games, and the never-ending, pull-the-string music boxes. She enjoys being taken for walks on sunny days, snatching heads off flowers as we pass, and she would splash and laugh forever in a warm bath or pool.

I've had my darling baby for nearly twenty years now, and, unless something happens, I guess I'll have her for another twenty years. She's been at the lovely seven- to nine-month stage for a long time, so I don't expect much change.

She still has a sweet baby face, innocent, unmarred by loss or disappointment or anger, and she still has her mass of blonde curls. But her hormones are those of a young woman—a plump, buxom, almost voluptuous young woman—and acne spoils her pretty face. Her hair, though darker now, is still her finest feature. How often I've had cause to be thankful for those lovely curls! People are usually uncomfortable, stuck for something to say, on first meeting my big baby, but they can always say, "What beautiful hair!"

And they do. It helps.

Others I know have a much harder time with their "forever" babies. Endless years with a fretful, crying child, every mealtime a turmoil of spitting resistance, all activity a cause of spasms and distress. Or a child with full mobility but never learning to heed "no" or "stop"; on the go all day every day, getting bigger and stronger with every year, being influenced by powerful adolescent hormones. And without the redeeming beautiful curls.

We met at a special playgroup, a group of young mothers coming to terms with the realization that our children were severely disabled. We talked through our guilt, our grief and disappointment, our anger, as we helped our babies to play, and we've kept in touch. Caring for a severely handicapped child is a big task, as is caring for a baby, but when supports are available it is not all-consuming.

We have had other children and been active in their lives, we've had part-time jobs while the children are in day care, our marriages have survived and we've had family holidays.

And we've become involved in "the field," working to ensure that the best possible services and supports are available for our children, and for other disabled people and their caregivers.

School councils, accommodation committees, fund-raising and fêtes, lobbying politicians, demonstrations and protests, and self-education—we've done it all, learning as we go. As our children reach nominal adult-hood, there are further decisions to be made, battles to be won. We need to be sure that there are suitable day activities available for them when the school system is no longer an option, and that appropriate long term accommodation will be provided when the time is right for them to leave our care.

For the most part, I've found people sensitive and helpful. Services and supports have been available when I have needed them, and the years have rolled by pretty smoothly.

But there have been jolts and hurts along the way. There was the ideologically pure occupational therapist, who removed my daughter's toys and music box from her wheelchair because they were "age-inappropriate." (I responded by tying a book, a chess set, and a rock music tape to her tray, and she banged and chewed them into oblivion.) Or the brutally honest doctor at the children's hospital who said, when I rushed her to the ER with croup, "I can admit her if you like, but she'd be better off at home. Children like that don't get the best treatment here." And the bastard who publicly queried my use of a disabled parking sticker (before the rules changed).

Dilemmas arise in the decisions I need to make on my daughter's behalf. As she reached puberty, I was offered, and accepted with misgivings, a hormone injection to stop her having periods. I think I secretly hoped it would stop her body from maturing: that I would be able to pretend forever that she was still a child. But it didn't and after a year or so I stopped the injections.

"Why should she wear a bra?" I wondered, until physical size provided an obvious answer. "What clothes should she wear?" I tend to dress her for her comfort and my convenience, but is this undermining her dignity as a young adult, denigrating her worth as a person? Should I dress her in the sort of things her sister wears: make an outlandish fashion statement on her behalf? What would she choose for herself if she could choose, and does it matter, since she has no concept of fashion or dignity? (These are issues one is made uncomfortably aware of, when working in the broader disability field.)

In deciding to seek an operation to stop her menstruating, was I motivated by her best interests or mine? (The Guardianship and Administration Board accepted that it would be in her best interests. Such important decisions are not made by caregivers alone.)

In years past, children such as ours would very likely have been placed in institutions at an early age. Parents of babies with much lesser disabilities were often advised not to take them home. "Put her in a home and forget you ever had her," they were told. And many did.

Recently I spent some time at a large institution, holding meetings with disabled people, their parents and their caregivers, and I observed a most amazing and moving phenomenon. The residents were in their thirties and had lived in the institution for more than twenty years. The staff was in daily contact with them and met all their physical needs. The parents visited from time to time. Yet, repeatedly, I was struck by the strength and durability of the emotional bond they had with their parents.

They couldn't get close enough, couldn't take their eyes off them, couldn't bear for the parent's attention to be anywhere but on them. An ungainly, non-verbal woman maneuvered laboriously along the table and sat on her father's knee, pressing her face to his. I felt so sad that these people had not been offered the encouragement and supports to keep their child at home for longer; to make the most of the love that was so obviously shared.

These days, fewer disabled children are born. Preventive immunization, genetic counseling, and improved obstetric care have contributed to this. Special tests early in pregnancy can identify many malformations or abnormalities, and parents can choose to have the pregnancy terminated. While very few people would choose to bring a severely disabled child into the world if they could avoid it, the implications of this newly acquired capacity to engineer a largely disability-free society need to be examined.

What message does it give to disabled members of our community about their worth, their right to exist and be supported? Will society refuse support for those families who knowingly give birth to a disabled child? Will even minor defects be eliminated, until only perfection is tolerated? And what will this mean for those whose disabilities or deformities could not be predicted, or are acquired after birth?

A friend of mine recently had tests early in her pregnancy, because in her first pregnancy the baby had been found to have a severe fetal defect, necessitating termination, and there was a chance this could recur. She was told these tests showed a different problem, Down syndrome, and that arrangements had been made for her to have a termination two days later.

She was offered no counseling about what having a child with Down syndrome would mean, or what factors she would need to consider in making her decision. It was not even appreciated that she had a decision to make! In fact, it was a very difficult decision for her, and only after a lot of heartbreak did she accept that she really could not manage a disabled child in her situation. The attitude to disability shown by her doctors is a little disturbing.

So. What am I saying in all this? There will always be children born with disabilities. And if it happens to you, it's not the end of the world—for you or your baby. No one can predict with certainty what path any child's development will follow. Or what sort of life he/she will be able to lead.

It will not be the life you dreamt about when you were expecting your baby, but it is his/her life. Having a disabled child makes you think about life: what it's for; what's important. And your ideas change quite a lot.

Your life won't be the one you were dreaming about either, but it will be a full life, a rich life. And it could have a lot of joy.

✦

FATHERS WITH DAUGHTERS

ONE OF THE things I've been struck by in my work is the great importance of fathers in shaping their daughters' self-esteem. I especially believe fathers should never put down their daughters' appearance even in "fun." Some men do this, perhaps out of some motive to "tidy them up" or make them more presentable. The effect is usually the complete reverse.

There are many good things dads can do. They can give praise. They can also enjoy joking and laughing with their daughters, developing their skills in conversation and repartee. Be alert to the fact that girls change and go through very different phases, so that what was once a good topic to joke about can become an acutely sensitive one that is better left alone.

Fathers are a source of social practice with the opposite sex. By conversing with their fathers about serious issues, by being admired for their minds as much as for their looks, girls learn to approach the opposite sex with the skills necessary to take the initiative and give as good as they get. They will never be bluffed or intimidated in male company.

They will also have the confidence to pick and choose their partner rather than being passive wallflowers.

CLOSE BUT SAFE

Fathers who are clear about not sexually invading their daughters can still be affectionate and warm—they don't have to get all uptight. Sexual touch and affectionate touch are totally distinct.

Having a strong marriage also helps your daughter's development—she sees a man and woman relating respectfully. If a daughter knows that her parents are close, then she will feel safer around her father, since his needs for affection and sexual partnership are clearly being met. For this reason, be wary of taking your daughter's side against your partner—if you have a problem with your partner, then deal with it on a one-on-one basis.

Respect is a key element between the genders and you as a father can model it. If you respect your daughter (and her mother) then she will insist on other males doing the same. If you put her down, she may allow other males to do so too, thinking this is normal. Being respectful is usually as simple as extending normal courtesy. For example, you can respect your daughter's developing need for privacy by asking permission to enter her room when she is inside.

BUILDING SELF-RELIANCE IN GIRLS

A FATHER CAN build some good independence skills with his daughter—teaching her about cars, fixing things, woodworking, dealing with money, going on trips or camping. In this way he'll know she's safer out in the real world, and less dependent.

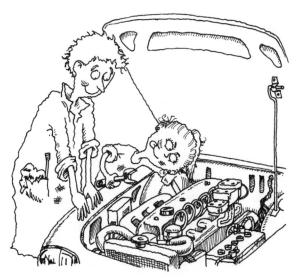

∿ seven ∿

Family Liberation

◆

At THE END of a book that has covered so much ground, I want to share a vision with you. It involves the big picture beyond our homes, but it applies to everything that happens within them. Something new is starting to happen in the world of the family—something that means we can begin to change the world we live in, without leaving our own neighborhoods to do it.

TIME FOR CHANGE

PARENTS HAVE NEVER had a real political voice—perhaps we're just too busy with little children to find the energy. It's as much as some of us can manage to crawl down to a voting booth every two or four years. But all this is starting to change at express-train speed.

Parents Are Angry

Having left the care of our world to politicians and technocrats, what have we ended up with?

Our world is so polluted that we sustain genetic damage, and have soaring rates of miscarriage and infertility. Asthma, a problem highly related to air quality, is now a problem for two in every five American children. Likewise with allergies and reactions to the chemical environment. Even the sunshine has become a danger.

Our world is violent because of inequity, and crushed families, and a media that promotes violence as a way of life.

The U.S. economy is unable to give meaningful or satisfying employment to men or teenagers, but it will employ young mothers, as long as they don't mind what kind of work they do or how poorly they are paid.

When it comes to politics—the "leadership" of the country—people want a better choice.

The Democratic and Republican dinosaurs have evolved to a very similar position—they demonstrate few real policy differences that ordinary people can get inspired about. The ends of the spectrum have moved to a boring middle—it could be argued that both are about economic rationalism, Yuppie values, and the dollar as the ultimate goal.

A Positive New Alliance

When there is so little choice and so much frustration, then a new alternative always emerges. In this case, it draws support (surprisingly) from both sides of the philosophical fence. An amazing new alliance is appearing in your neighborhood—between stereotyped groups such as the alternative-lifestyle, high-tech environmentalists, and the right-wing, family-oriented, Christian traditionalists.

This is leading to all kinds of beautiful breakouts from the old stereotypes. When I give lecture tours in Australia, I am meeting at the same gatherings highly responsible, monogamous, and hard-working "hippies"—side by side with straight-backed churchgoers who hug their children, renounce smacking, belong to Amnesty International, and boycott Nestlé!

THE WAY FORWARD

I BELIEVE THAT more and more parents are working positively toward a world that embraces serenity, compassion, free-spiritedness, and happiness.

In fact, I don't think it is too optimistic to say that a kind of parent power is emerging. It will include and be merged with the green movement, because parents and children are natural environmentalists. It will embrace the social, political, and economic equality of the sexes, because parents want a good future for both boys and girls, and it will support moves to advance gender relationships. It will make a huge difference to the shape of the twenty-first century.

So to end this book, here is a suggested manifesto.

A Statement of Beliefs to ↶ Guide Actions in Family ↷ Liberation

+ Nothing is more important than raising healthy, happy children.
+ No one can or should raise children alone. We all need each other's help.
+ In particular we need a society that takes parents' needs very seriously, and funds those needs, in return for the gift we give back of healthy, contributing adults.
+ The best way to make children safe is to take more care of parents.
+ The best way to deprogram our overscheduled children is to deprogram ourselves.
+ Parents are responsible to their children—for not smoking around them, for fastening their seat belts, for protecting them from abuse. Kids are not property.
+ We must work at allowing children to hang on to childhood as long as possible.
+ We must work to increase the positive contact between children and adults. This means abandoning smacking and fighting sexual abuse, but it also means showing people better ways of connecting with their kids.
+ We have to become active mentors to younger peo-

ple, helping young parents, caring for other people's children, so as to spread the load of raising our young from the overburdened nuclear family into something we haven't had for a long time—real community.

✦ We have to have family-friendly workplaces, guaranteed by legislation, where fathers and mothers can fit work around their families' needs, instead of having to choose between career and family.

✦ The concept of family must be broadened to include everyone—single, gay, childless, divorced, elderly, criminal, refugee, businessman, homeless teenager.

We have to put our arms around everyone and say, "Welcome home!"

✦

Resources

✦

HERE ARE SOME national organizations you can contact for information and guidance on a variety of parenting issues:

National Education Association
1201 16th Street, N.W.
Washington, D.C. 20036
T: (202) 833-4000
Website: www.nea.org

National 4H Headquarters
1400 Independence Avenue, S.W.
Washington, D.C. 20250
Website: www.national4-hheadquarters.gov

National Parent Information Network
Children's Research Center
51 Gerty Drive
Champaign, IL 61820
T: (800) 583-4135
Website: www.npin.org

Child Welfare League of America
440 First Street N.W., 3rd floor
Washington, D.C. 20001
T: (202) 638-2952
Website: www.cwla.org

Family First
P.O. Box 2882
Tampa, FL 33601
T: (813) 222-8300
Website: www.familyfirst.net

Zero to Three: National Center for Infants, Toddlers, and Families
734 15th Street, N.W.
Suite 1000
Washington, D.C. 20005
T: (202) 638-1144
Website: www.zerotothree.org

U.S. Department of Education
400 Maryland Avenue, S.W.
Washington, D.C. 20202
T: (888) 814-6252
Website: www.nochildleftbehind.gov

We also especially recommend *Mothering* magazine. To subscribe, call (800) 984-8116 or write P.O. Box 1690, Santa Fe, NM, 87504. We find this a great source of inspiration.

Play groups are a wonderful place to play and make friends. Your children will like them too! Seriously, play groups are get-togethers for children under school age and their parents, which help them learn to play together, and help you meet other parents in your area. They are in almost every suburb and town. Recently, dads' play groups have begun forming. Look up play groups in your local phone book or on the Web to find the one nearest you.

About the Authors

✦

Steve AND SHAARON BIDDULPH are the parents of two children (ages sixteen and nine), and Steve has been a family psychologist for over twenty years. Steve lectures around the world on childhood subjects and is the author of five other books, including *The Secret of Happy Children, The Secret Life of Men,* and *Raising Boys.* The Biddulphs live in New South Wales, Australia, and the United Kingdom.